D1252378

SOUPS AND STEWS

Canadian Living's *best*

BY

Elizabeth Baird

AND

The Food Writers of Canadian Living® Magazine
and The Canadian Living Test Kitchen

A MADISON PRESS BOOK
PRODUCED FOR
BALLANTINE BOOKS AND CANADIAN LIVING

Ballantine Books
A Division of
Random House of
Canada Limited
1265 Aerowood Drive
Mississauga, Ontario
Canada
L4W 1B9

Canadian Living
Telemedia
Communications Inc.
25 Sheppard Avenue West
Suite 100
North York, Ontario
Canada
M2N 6S7

Canadian Cataloguing in Publication Data

Baird, Elizabeth
Canadian Living's best soups and stews

(Canadian Living's best)
"A Madison Press Book".
Produced for Ballantine Books and Canadian Living.
ISBN 0-345-39852-1

1. Soups. 2. Stews. I. Title. II. Title: Soups and stews. III. Series.

TX757.B34 1997   641.8'13   C97-931462-3

EDITORIAL DIRECTOR: Hugh Brewster
PROJECT EDITOR: Wanda Nowakowska
EDITORIAL ASSISTANCE: Beverley Renahan
PRODUCTION DIRECTOR: Susan Barrable
PRODUCTION COORDINATOR: Donna Chong
BOOK DESIGN AND LAYOUT: Gordon Sibley Design Inc.
COLOR SEPARATION: Colour Technologies
PRINTING AND BINDING: St. Joseph Printing Limited

CANADIAN LIVING ADVISORY BOARD: Elizabeth Baird, Bonnie Baker Cowan,
Anna Hobbs, Caren King

CANADIAN LIVING'S BEST SOUPS AND STEWS
was produced by Madison Press Books
which is under the direction of Albert E. Cummings

Madison Press Books
40 Madison Avenue
Toronto, Ontario, Canada
M5R 2S1

Printed in Canada

Contents

Strawberry Melon Soup (p. 30)

Coconut Curried Chicken Stew (p. 48)

Chunky Mushroom Soup (p. 16)

Introduction

Soups and stews have a particularly warm spot in my heart — partly, I suppose, because I couldn't survive our chilly Canadian autumns, downright cold winters and (unfortunately!) chilly springs without them.

But the truth is, a love for this easy-to-make, relaxed sort of food is bred in the bones. Who can resist the aromas of onions, garlic, herbs and spices wafting through the house, building anticipation for a pot of real chicken noodle soup, a fish-flecked chowder, a saucy chicken cacciatore or a rich brown curry?

Soups and stews are easy on the cook, too. A few minutes of work peeling, chopping and browning leads into the laziest cooking method going — a slow simmer, with time to do other things while supper bubbles away in the pot. Best of all, the most economical cuts of meat, seafood and poultry conspire with bargain vegetables to keep costs to a minimum while delivering the maximum in satisfaction. And because most soups and stews are make-ahead, they taste even better when chilled overnight and then reheated to bring out their rich, mellowed flavors. They're also a delicious guarantee of supper on the table, no matter how hectic your schedule.

But not all soups and stews are the hearty rib-stickers of yesteryear. In *Canadian Living's Best Soups and Stews*, we've adapted recipes to appeal to today's health-conscious cooks — with leaner cuts of meat; less oil, cream and butter; and cooking methods that encourage you to take off poultry skin, trim and skim off fat and make the most of grains, such as barley and rice, and healthful vegetables including broccoli, tomatoes, carrots, squash and sweet potato.

And for those brief weeks when it finally warms up here in northern North America, we've included a refreshing selection of summer-perfect fruit and vegetable soups that you can whizz up in minutes in the blender or food processor.

Welcome to the pleasures of soup-and-stew cooking!

Elizabeth Baird

Greek Lamb and Bean Stew (recipe, p. 77)

All The Best Soups

Soup is body-and-soul food. When a chill is in the air, soup bowls are brimming with hearty lentils, smoky flavors, nose-tweaking aromas, vegetables galore and real contentment. Come the warmer months, soup lightens up to refresh but still to sustain and satisfy with the season's tenderest vegetables and juiciest fruits.

Hearty Baked Ribollita ▶

Soup? Yes — but baked with slices of good sourdough bread, this rustic Italian soup scoops up almost like a casserole. And, it's guaranteed to ward off the worst bluster of winter.

Per serving: about
- 440 calories
- 16 g fat
- excellent source of calcium and iron
- 21 g protein
- 54 g carbohydrate
- very high source of fiber

1/2 oz	dried porcini mushrooms	15 g
1 tbsp	olive oil	15 mL
3 oz	pancetta or bacon, chopped	90 g
1	onion, chopped	1
2	cloves garlic, minced	2
3	carrots, diced	3
1	stalk celery, diced	1
1-1/2 cups	chopped fennel or cabbage	375 mL
1 cup	cubed peeled potato	250 mL
1 tsp	dried thyme	5 mL
1/2 tsp	each dried sage and pepper	2 mL
4 cups	chicken or vegetable stock	1 L
1	can (28 oz/796 mL) tomatoes, chopped	1
1 tbsp	red wine vinegar	15 mL
1	can (19 oz/540 mL) white kidney beans, drained and rinsed	1
4 cups	finely chopped kale	1 L
6 slices	stale Italian bread	6
3/4 cup	freshly grated Parmesan or pecorino cheese	175 mL

● In small bowl, cover mushrooms with 1/2 cup (125 mL) warm water; let stand for 20 minutes. Drain mushrooms, reserving liquid; chop mushrooms coarsely and set aside. Strain liquid through cheesecloth-lined sieve into clean bowl; set aside.

● Meanwhile, in large heavy saucepan, heat oil over medium heat; cook pancetta, stirring, for 5 minutes or until softened. Add onion, garlic, carrots, celery, fennel, potato, thyme, sage and pepper; cook, stirring, for 10 minutes or until softened.

● Stir in chicken stock, tomatoes, vinegar and reserved mushrooms and soaking liquid; bring to boil. Reduce heat and simmer for 20 minutes. Stir in kidney beans and kale; simmer until kale is wilted and tender. *(Ribollita can be prepared to this point, cooled, covered and refrigerated for up to 24 hours.)*

● Ladle soup into 13- x 9-inch (3 L) baking dish. Arrange bread in layer on top; sprinkle with Parmesan cheese. Cover and bake in 350°F (180°C) oven for 30 minutes. Uncover and bake for 15 to 20 minutes longer or until bubbling and top is crusty and golden. Makes 6 servings.

Supper Squash and Bean Soup ◄

4 oz	thickly sliced lean prosciutto	125 g
2 tbsp	olive oil	25 mL
3	onions, chopped	3
1	stalk celery, diced	1
4	cloves garlic, minced	4
1	small butternut squash (1-3/4 lb/875 g)	1
8 cups	chicken stock	2 L
1	sweet red pepper	1
4 cups	shredded collards	1 L
2 cups	cooked white kidney beans	500 mL
1 tbsp	chopped fresh sage	15 mL
1/2 cup	black olives	125 mL
3/4 cup	freshly grated Parmesan or pecorino cheese	175 mL

● Cut prosciutto into matchstick-size strips. In large heavy saucepan or stockpot, heat oil over medium heat; cook onions, celery, garlic and prosciutto, stirring often, for about 8 minutes or until softened.

● Meanwhile, peel and seed squash; cut into bite-size chunks. Add to pan along with chicken stock; bring to boil. Reduce heat, cover and simmer for 10 minutes or until squash is tender.

● Meanwhile, core and seed red pepper; cut in half crosswise, then into thin strips. Add to soup along with collards, kidney beans and sage; cook for 3 minutes or until red pepper is tender. Remove from heat; stir in olives. Ladle into warmed bowls; sprinkle with cheese. Makes 6 servings.

*H*ere's supper in a bowl, with lots of vegetables — squash, red pepper and collards — plus the substance of beans and the richness that a few slices of prosciutto and a sprinkle of cheese offer.

Per serving: about
- 355 calories
- 14 g fat
- excellent source of calcium and iron
- 23 g protein
- 38 g carbohydrate
- very high source of fiber

TIP: You can substitute spinach or Swiss chard for the collards; add along with the olives.

Scaramouche Black Bean Soup

2 cups	dried black beans	500 mL
8 oz	slab double-smoked bacon	250 g
2 tbsp	butter	25 mL
1	large onion, sliced	1
2	cans (10 oz/284 mL each) chicken broth	2
	LIME CORIANDER CREAM	
1/2 cup	sour cream	125 mL
2 tbsp	finely chopped fresh coriander	25 mL
2 tbsp	lime juice	25 mL
2	tomatoes, seeded and diced	2

● In large saucepan, soak beans in 6 cups (1.5 L) cold water for 8 hours. (Or, bring to boil and boil for 2 minutes; cover and let stand for 1 hour.) Drain and rinse beans.

● In large saucepan, bring beans and 12 cups (3 L) cold water to boil; reduce heat, cover and simmer for about 1 hour or until just tender. Drain and rinse.

● Trim tough bottom rind off bacon; reserve rind and dice remaining bacon. In large heavy saucepan, cook diced bacon over medium heat, stirring often, for about 15 minutes or until softened. Drain off fat; set bacon aside.

● Add butter to pan and melt over medium heat; cook onion for 5 minutes or until softened. Add beans, cooked bacon, reserved bacon rind, chicken broth and 3 cups (750 mL) water; bring to boil. Reduce heat and simmer for 40 minutes or until bacon and beans are tender. Discard bacon rind.

● Transfer soup, in batches, to food processor or blender; purée until smooth. Return to saucepan and heat through.

● LIME CORIANDER CREAM: In bowl, combine sour cream, coriander and lime juice. Ladle soup into warmed bowls; spoon cream on soup and sprinkle with tomatoes. Makes 8 servings.

*C*hef Keith Froggett served bowlfuls of this smoky soup at a recent fundraising event at Toronto's Gardiner Museum of Ceramic Art. A chunk of rind-on, double-smoked bacon is essential to the recipe. Look for it at a good deli or butcher shop.

Per serving: about
- 290 calories
- 10 g fat
- good source of iron
- 17 g protein
- 34 g carbohydrate
- very high source of fiber

Barley Vegetable Soup ▶

Naomi Duguid and Jeffrey Alford, award-winning food writers and husband and wife, created this wintertime comfort soup.

Per serving: about
- 250 calories
- 5 g protein
- 4 g fat
- 50 g carbohydrate
- good source of iron
- very high source of fiber

1 tbsp	olive oil	15 mL
1	onion, chopped	1
3 cups	sliced mushrooms (8 oz/250 g)	750 mL
3/4 cup	pearl barley	175 mL
6 cups	vegetable or chicken stock	1.5 L
2	bay leaves	2
1/4 tsp	pepper	1 mL
3 cups	diced peeled potatoes	750 mL
1-1/2 cups	diced carrots	375 mL
1/2 tsp	salt	2 mL
1/2 cup	freshly grated Parmesan or shredded Cheddar cheese (optional)	125 mL
1/4 cup	chopped fresh parsley	50 mL

● In large heavy saucepan, heat oil over medium heat; cook onion, stirring often, for 2 to 3 minutes or until softened. Add mushrooms; cook, stirring often, for about 5 minutes or until softened. Add barley; cook, stirring, for 1 minute.

● Add vegetable stock, 2 cups (500 mL) water, bay leaves and pepper; bring to boil. Reduce heat to medium-low; cover and simmer for 1 hour.

● Add potatoes, carrots and salt; return to boil. Reduce heat to medium-low; simmer for 30 minutes or until vegetables are tender. Discard bay leaves. Ladle into warmed bowls; sprinkle with Parmesan (if using) and parsley. Makes 5 servings.

TIP: If desired, soak 1/2 oz (15 g) dried porcini mushrooms (see p. 6). Drain, reserving liquid; rinse and chop. Add to soup along with soaking liquid and barley.

Speedy Tomato Bean Soup

End of the week and the fridge is looking bare? A cupboard stocked with beans and tomatoes can send out a lifeline and rescue the supper hour with a very substantial and delicious soup.

Per serving: about
- 240 calories
- 12 g protein
- 4 g fat
- 42 g carbohydrate
- excellent source of iron
- very high source of fiber

2 tsp	vegetable oil	10 mL
3	cloves garlic, minced	3
2	onions, chopped	2
2	carrots, diced	2
1/2 tsp	chili powder	2 mL
1/4 tsp	pepper	1 mL
1	can (28 oz/796 mL) tomatoes	1
2 cups	vegetable stock	500 mL
1	can (19 oz/540 mL) black beans or chick-peas, drained and rinsed	1
1 tbsp	tomato paste	15 mL
1/4 cup	shredded old Cheddar cheese (optional)	50 mL

● In large heavy saucepan, heat oil over medium heat; add garlic, onions, carrots, chili powder and pepper. Cover and cook, stirring occasionally, for about 8 minutes or until onions are softened.

● Add tomatoes, breaking up with fork. Add vegetable stock, black beans, tomato paste and 1 cup (250 mL) water; bring to boil. Reduce heat and simmer for 15 minutes or until carrots are tender. Ladle into warmed bowls; sprinkle with Cheddar (if using). Makes 4 servings.

White Bean Soup

Beans are a stellar way to bulk up the fiber and cut down on fat in the diet. Puréed in soup, they provide a voluptuous texture like the one usually provided by cream.

Per serving: about
- 205 calories
- 10 g protein
- 5 g fat
- 32 g carbohydrate
- good source of iron
- very high source of fiber

1 tbsp	olive oil	15 mL
2	cloves garlic, minced	2
2	onions, chopped	2
2	stalks celery, diced	2
1 tsp	dried thyme	5 mL
1/2 tsp	pepper	2 mL
3-1/2 cups	vegetable or chicken stock	875 mL
1	can (19 oz/540 mL) white pea (navy) beans or kidney beans, drained and rinsed	1
1/2 tsp	grated lemon rind	2 mL
2 tsp	lemon juice	10 mL
2	green onions, finely chopped	2
2 tbsp	chopped fresh basil	25 mL

● In large heavy saucepan, heat oil over medium heat; cook garlic, onions, celery, thyme and pepper, stirring, for 2 minutes. Reduce heat to medium-low; cover and cook, stirring often, for about 15 minutes or until softened. Stir in vegetable stock and beans; bring to boil. Reduce heat and simmer for 5 minutes.

● Transfer soup, in batches, to food processor or blender; purée until smooth. Return to saucepan; stir in lemon rind, lemon juice and green onions. Cook over medium heat until steaming. Ladle into warmed bowls; sprinkle with basil. Makes 4 servings.

TIP: You can substitute 2 tbsp (25 mL) chopped fresh coriander, mint, dill or parsley for the basil.

Quick Chili Soup

Bulgur gives a ground-meat texture to this chock-full-of-vegetables soup.

Per serving: about
- 190 calories
- 7 g protein
- 5 g fat
- 32 g carbohydrate
- good source of iron
- very high source of fiber

2 tbsp	vegetable oil	25 mL
2 tbsp	chili powder	25 mL
2 tsp	each dried oregano and basil	10 mL
1 tsp	each ground cumin and salt	5 mL
Pinch	cayenne pepper	Pinch
2	onions, chopped	2
3	carrots, chopped	3
1	sweet green pepper, chopped	1
5 cups	diced eggplant (2 small Japanese or 1 large)	1.25 L
1 cup	sliced mushrooms	250 mL
1/3 cup	bulgur	75 mL
1/4 cup	tomato paste	50 mL
1	can (28 oz/796 mL) tomatoes, chopped	1
1	can (19 oz/540 mL) chick-peas or red kidney or black beans, or black-eyed peas, drained and rinsed	1
2 tsp	Worcestershire sauce	10 mL
2 tsp	lemon juice	10 mL

● In large heavy saucepan, heat oil over medium heat. Add chili powder, oregano, basil, cumin, salt and cayenne pepper; cook, stirring, for 1 minute. Add onions, carrots, green pepper, eggplant and mushrooms; cook, stirring often, for about 10 minutes or until softened.

● Stir in bulgur, tomato paste and tomatoes. Add 8 cups (2 L) water and chick-peas; bring to boil, stirring often. Reduce heat and simmer gently for 25 minutes or until bulgur is tender. Stir in Worcestershire sauce and lemon juice. Makes 8 servings.

TIP: Serve topped with crumbled corn tortilla chips and a dollop of thick yogurt or no-fat sour cream. Or, sprinkle with shredded Monterey Jack cheese and diced sweet green pepper or avocado.

Outward Bound Reunion Soup

8 cups	chicken stock	2 L
1 cup	green lentils	250 mL
1/4 cup	brown rice	50 mL
1/4 cup	bulgur	50 mL
1/4 cup	tomato paste	50 mL
2 tbsp	vegetable oil	25 mL
2	onions, chopped	2
1 tbsp	curry powder	15 mL
2 tsp	cinnamon	10 mL
1/2 tsp	each ginger, nutmeg and pepper	2 mL
1 cup	roasted peanuts	250 mL
1/4 cup	sesame seeds	50 mL

● In large heavy saucepan, combine chicken stock, lentils, rice, bulgur and tomato paste; bring to boil. Reduce heat to low; cover and simmer for about 25 minutes or until rice and lentils are tender but not mushy.

● Meanwhile, in large skillet, heat oil over medium heat; cook onions, curry powder, cinnamon, ginger, nutmeg and pepper, stirring often, for about 10 minutes or until onions are tender.

● Add peanuts and sesame seeds; cook, stirring often, for 2 minutes. Add to rice mixture; bring to simmer. Makes 8 servings.

First simmered over a campfire on a cold and rainy September night, this hearty soup is always served whenever Elizabeth Baird's group of Outward Bounders gets together.

Per serving: about
- 345 calories
- 17 g fat
- excellent source of iron
- 19 g protein
- 32 g carbohydrate
- very high source of fiber

Split Pea and Ham Soup

2 cups	dried split peas (1 lb/500 g)	500 mL
1	smoked ham hock	1
1 cup	chopped onion	250 mL
1 cup	finely chopped carrots	250 mL
1/2 cup	chopped celery (with leaves)	125 mL
3/4 tsp	pepper	4 mL
1/4 tsp	ground cloves	1 mL
1	bay leaf	1
1-1/4 tsp	salt	6 mL

● In large heavy saucepan, bring peas and 12 cups (3 L) water to boil; remove from heat and let stand for 1 hour. Skim off any foam.

● Add ham hock, onion, carrots, celery, pepper, cloves and bay leaf; bring to boil. Reduce heat and simmer for about 2 hours or until peas are tender. Season with salt.

● Remove ham hock; remove and discard skin, fat and bone. Chop meat and return to soup. Discard bay leaf. Makes 8 servings.

TIP: You can use a ham bone, with any meat clinging to it, instead of a ham hock, or 12 oz (375 g) smoked sausage.

Some classics live on to be enjoyed generation after generation. This is one such classic in the soup world and, like a lot of soups, it's delicious — some say even more delicious — the day after it's been made.

Per serving: about
- 245 calories
- 4 g fat
- good source of iron
- 18 g protein
- 36 g carbohydrate
- very high source of fiber

THE RIGHT POT FOR SOUPS

A deep tall pot, called a stockpot, is the best, especially if the pot has a heavy bottom; an enclosed aluminum pad, or sandwich, is ideal. This sandwich distributes heat evenly and avoids burning the beginnings of many soups — aromatic vegetables and herbs cooked over low heat in oil. A stockpot is also very useful when making stock, which often calls for more liquid than your usual saucepan will hold, or for cooking pasta.

Squash Soup with Chili Paint ▼

Bonnie Stern obtained the recipe for this vivid soup from Banff's Buffalo Mountain Lodge where regional food enthusiast Hubert Aumeier wears the chef's whites.

Per serving: about
- 190 calories
- 5 g fat
- high source of fiber
- 7 g protein
- 32 g carbohydrate

2 tbsp	butter, softened	25 mL
2	butternut squash (2 lb/1 kg each)	2
1	onion, diced	1
1	sweet potato, peeled and diced	1
6 cups	chicken stock (approx)	1.5 L
1 tsp	chopped fresh thyme (or pinch dried)	5 mL
1/2 tsp	salt	2 mL
1/4 tsp	pepper	1 mL
	CHILI PAINT	
3	dried ancho chilies	3
1/3 cup	chicken stock	75 mL
1/4 cup	sour cream	50 mL

● CHILI PAINT: Roast chilies on baking sheet in 400°F (200°C) oven for 1 to 2 minutes or until pliable. Open chilies; discard ribs and seeds. Place in bowl and cover with boiling water; let stand for 20 minutes. Drain well. In blender, purée chilies with chicken stock; stir in sour cream. Strain through sieve into bowl; set aside.

● Meanwhile, line baking sheet with foil; brush lightly with some of the butter. Cut squash in half; scrape out seeds. Place, cut side down, on prepared pan. Roast in 350°F (180°C) oven for 1 hour or until very tender. Scoop out flesh; set aside.

● In large heavy saucepan, melt remaining butter over medium heat; cook onion and sweet potato, stirring occasionally, for 5 minutes or until onion is softened and fragrant. Add chicken stock; bring to boil. Add squash; cook, stirring occasionally, for 15 to 20 minutes or until sweet potatoes are tender.

● Transfer soup, in batches, to blender or food processor; purée until smooth. Return to pan; add thyme, salt and pepper. Thin with more stock or water if desired. Ladle into warmed bowls. Using squeeze bottle or spoon, drizzle chili paint in decorative pattern over soup. Make 8 servings.

Gingery Sweet Potato Soup

6 cups	cubed peeled sweet potatoes (about 3 large)	1.5 L
3-1/2 cups	chicken stock	875 mL
1 tbsp	minced gingerroot	15 mL
1/2 cup	unsweetened coconut milk	125 mL
3 tbsp	lime juice	50 mL
1/2 tsp	salt	2 mL
1/4 tsp	pepper	1 mL
1/4 cup	sliced almonds, toasted	50 mL
1/4 cup	chopped fresh coriander	50 mL

● In large heavy saucepan, bring potatoes, chicken stock and ginger to boil; reduce heat, cover and simmer for about 10 minutes or until potatoes are tender.

● Transfer soup, in batches, to food processor or blender; purée until smooth. Return to saucepan; stir in coconut milk, lime juice, salt and pepper. Cook over low heat just until heated through. Ladle into warmed bowls; sprinkle with almonds and coriander. Makes 8 servings.

Ginger, lime juice and coconut milk complement the mellow flavor of sweet potatoes. For a thinner consistency, increase stock.

Per serving: about
- 120 calories
- 4 g protein
- 6 g fat
- 14 g carbohydrate

Potato Garlic Vichyssoise

1 tbsp	butter	15 mL
3	cloves garlic, slivered	3
2	leeks, sliced	2
4 cups	diced peeled potatoes	1 L
4 cups	chicken or vegetable stock	1 L
1 cup	2% evaporated milk	250 mL
1 tbsp	lemon juice	15 mL
1/4 tsp	hot pepper sauce	1 mL
1/4 cup	chopped fresh dill (or 1 tsp/5 mL dried dillweed)	50 mL

● In large heavy saucepan, melt butter over medium-low heat; cook garlic, leeks and potatoes, stirring often, for 5 minutes.

● Pour in chicken stock; bring to simmer. Cover and cook for 15 minutes or until vegetables are very tender.

● Transfer soup, in batches, to blender or food processor; purée until smooth. Return to saucepan; stir in milk, lemon juice and hot pepper sauce. Heat through; stir in dill. Makes 4 servings.

Normally a chilled soup, vichyssoise is just as delicious hot, especially with a few added touches of garlic, lemon juice and dill.

Per serving: about
- 260 calories
- 13 g protein
- 6 g fat
- 41 g carbohydrate
- good source of calcium

Orchard and Garden Soup

1-1/2 cups	chopped onions	375 mL
1 cup	chopped celery	250 mL
1	potato, peeled and chopped	1
1	cucumber, peeled, seeded and chopped	1
1	large tart apple, peeled and chopped	1
3 cups	chicken stock	750 mL
1/2 cup	milk or 18% cream	125 mL
1/2 tsp	curry powder	2 mL
	Salt and pepper	
	Chopped fresh chives	

● In large heavy saucepan, combine onions, celery, potato, cucumber, apple and chicken stock; bring to boil. Reduce heat, cover and simmer for 30 minutes or until vegetables are softened.

● Transfer soup, in batches, to food processor or blender; purée until smooth. Return to saucepan; stir in milk, curry powder, and salt and pepper to taste. Heat soup until steaming. Ladle into warmed bowls; sprinkle with chives. Makes 8 servings.

From Quebec orchardist Carol Petch comes this curry-kissed apple and vegetable smoothie.

Per serving: about
- 70 calories
- 3 g protein
- 1 g fat
- 13 g carbohydrate

Chunky Mushroom Soup ▶

A *selection of exotic mushrooms — crimini, shiitake and frilly oyster varieties — boost the woodsiness of regular agaricus mushroom soup. Potato serves as an interesting way to thicken a soup.*

Per serving: about
- 185 calories
- 5 g protein
- 8 g fat
- 24 g carbohydrate
- good source of iron
- high source of fiber

5 cups	vegetable or chicken stock	1.25 L
1	potato, peeled and cubed	1
12 oz	fresh exotic mushrooms (crimini, shiitake, oyster)	375 g
8 oz	button mushrooms	250 g
2 tbsp	vegetable oil	25 mL
2	onions, finely chopped	2
2	cloves garlic, minced	2
2	carrots, finely chopped	2
1/2 tsp	dried thyme	2 mL
1/4 tsp	each paprika and pepper	1 mL
2 tbsp	sherry	25 mL

● In small saucepan, bring 1-1/2 cups (375 mL) of the vegetable stock to boil. Add potato; cover and cook over medium heat for about 10 minutes or until tender. Pour into blender or food processor; purée until smooth. Set aside.

● Meanwhile, trim and slice exotic and button mushrooms; set aside.

● In large heavy saucepan, heat oil over medium heat; cook onions, garlic and carrots, stirring occasionally, for 5 minutes or until softened.

● Stir in exotic and button mushrooms, thyme, paprika and pepper; cook, stirring often, for about 20 minutes or until mushrooms start to turn golden and no liquid remains.

● Stir in potato purée and remaining stock; bring to boil. Reduce heat and simmer for 5 minutes. Stir in sherry; simmer for 2 minutes. Makes 4 servings.

TIP: Shiitake mushrooms have tough stems which should be removed before mushrooms are cooked.

Quick Mushroom Soup

Y*ou don't need many mushrooms to make this easy and impressive soup.*

Per serving: about
- 170 calories
- 10 g protein
- 6 g fat
- 19 g carbohydrate
- good source of iron

1 tbsp	butter	15 mL
1	onion, chopped	1
4 cups	sliced mushrooms (about 10 oz/285 g)	1 L
1/4 cup	all-purpose flour	50 mL
3 cups	chicken stock	750 mL
1	bay leaf	1
Pinch	dried thyme	Pinch
1/3 cup	2% evaporated milk	75 mL
1/4 cup	sliced green onions	50 mL

● In large heavy saucepan, melt butter over medium heat; cook onion, stirring often, for 3 minutes. Add mushrooms; cook for about 5 minutes or until tender and juicy. Sprinkle with flour; cook, stirring, for 1 minute or until juice is absorbed.

● Stir in chicken stock, bay leaf and thyme until blended. Bring to boil; reduce heat and simmer for 15 minutes.

● Stir in milk; return to simmer. Discard bay leaf. Ladle into warmed bowls; sprinkle with green onions. Makes 3 servings.

Garlic Soup with Croûtes

Fear not the amount of garlic in this clear broth soup. The sharp edges of the so-called stinking rose always smooth out and sweeten when cooked.

Per serving: about
- 210 calories
- 7 g fat
- 10 g protein
- 26 g carbohydrate

14	cloves garlic	14
2	each sprigs fresh parsley and thyme	2
4	fresh sage leaves	4
2	cans (each 10 oz/284 mL) chicken broth	2
3-1/2 cups	water	875 L
	CROÛTES	
1	clove garlic, halved	1
4	slices day-old sourdough country loaf	4
1 tbsp	olive oil	15 mL
1/4 cup	shredded Gruyère cheese	50 mL

● Peel skin from garlic. On cutting board and using flat side of large knife, smash cloves to crush. Place in large heavy saucepan.

● Add parsley, thyme, sage, chicken broth and water; bring to boil. Reduce heat, cover and simmer for 30 minutes. Strain through fine sieve into large bowl.

● CROÛTES: Rub cut sides of garlic over bread. Brush both sides of bread with oil; sprinkle cheese evenly over one side. Broil for 1 to 2 minutes or until cheese is melted and bubbly. Place each in soup bowl. Ladle soup over croûtes. Makes 4 servings.

TIP: Croûtes, cheese-topped bread slices, are a bonus for many soups. You can either put them in the bottom of the soup bowl before filling, or float them on top. It's important to get a bread that holds its structure when wet, and for this, we cannot emphasize too much the importance of authentic, chewy sourdough bread.

French Onion Soup

Cooking the onions slowly with a touch of sugar caramelizes them, and that's the flavor secret of this super-simple French classic.

Per serving: about
- 255 calories
- 10 g fat
- good source of calcium
- 13 g protein
- 28 g carbohydrate

2	onions	2
1 tbsp	butter	15 mL
1	clove garlic, finely chopped	1
2 tsp	granulated sugar	10 mL
1/2 tsp	dried marjoram	2 mL
1/2 tsp	pepper	2 mL
Pinch	salt	Pinch
4 cups	beef stock	1 L
1 tbsp	balsamic or red wine vinegar	15 mL
4	slices French bread	4
3/4 cup	shredded Swiss cheese	175 mL

● Cut onions in half lengthwise; cut crosswise into thin slices. In large heavy saucepan, melt butter over medium heat. Add onions, garlic, sugar, marjoram, pepper and salt; reduce heat to medium-low, cover and cook, stirring occasionally, for 15 to 20 minutes or until onions are limp and colored.

● Pour in beef stock and vinegar; bring to boil. Reduce heat to medium; simmer for 10 minutes.

● Meanwhile, toast bread until golden brown. Place four ovenproof soup bowls on baking sheet; ladle soup into bowls. Top with toast; sprinkle cheese evenly over top. Broil for about 3 minutes or until cheese is bubbly and golden. Makes 4 servings.

Quick and Easy Root Soup

6 cups	chicken or vegetable stock	1.5 L
1-1/2 cups	coarsely chopped onions	375 mL
1/2 cup	sliced celery	125 mL
1 lb	parsnips or carrots, peeled and chopped (about 8)	500 g
1/2 tsp	finely grated orange rind	2 mL
1/4 tsp	grated nutmeg	1 mL
1/4 tsp	pepper	1 mL
1/3 cup	chopped fresh chives, parsley, chervil or coriander	75 mL

● In large heavy saucepan, combine chicken stock, onions, celery and parsnips; cover and bring to boil. Reduce heat and simmer for about 30 minutes or until vegetables are tender.

● Transfer soup, in batches, to food processor or blender; purée until smooth. Return to saucepan. Add orange rind, nutmeg and pepper; bring to simmer. Ladle into warmed bowls; sprinkle with chives. Makes 8 servings.

Either carrots or parsnips — two fine, inexpensive fall and winter roots — cook up quickly into an amazingly good soup.

Per serving: about
● 80 calories
● 1 g fat
● 5 g protein
● 13 g carbohydrate

Cream of Asparagus

1-1/2 lb	asparagus	750 g
2 tbsp	butter	25 mL
1	leek (white part only), chopped	1
1 tbsp	chopped fresh parsley	15 mL
1 tsp	grated lemon rind	5 mL
2 tsp	lemon juice	10 mL
1/4 tsp	pepper	1 mL
4 cups	vegetable or chicken stock	1 L
1/2 cup	10% cream	125 mL

● Snap tough ends off asparagus; starting at tips, cut stalks into 1-1/2-inch (4 cm) pieces. Set aside.

● In large heavy saucepan, melt butter over medium heat; cook leek, stirring occasionally, for about 10 minutes or until very soft. Add asparagus, parsley, lemon rind, lemon juice and pepper. Pour in vegetable stock; bring to boil. Reduce heat and simmer for 5 minutes or until asparagus is tender. Using tongs, remove 1 cup (250 mL) of the asparagus tips; chop coarsely and set aside.

● Transfer soup, in batches, to blender or food processor; purée until smooth. Press through fine sieve over saucepan to remove any fiber. Pour in cream; heat until steaming. Ladle into warmed bowls; garnish with reserved chopped asparagus. Makes 6 servings.

TIP: A regular cooking onion can replace the leek in this and many other soup or stew recipes.

If asparagus says spring, then asparagus soup says crowd-pleasing spring entertaining.

Per serving: about
● 95 calories
● 7 g fat
● 3 g protein
● 7 g carbohydrate

Corn and Bacon Chowder

Old-fashioned, yes, and timeless too — this quick, sustaining soup comes from the rich farmlands of southern Ontario.

Per serving: about
- 220 calories
- 6 g fat
- 10 g protein
- 33 g carbohydrate

6	strips lean bacon, chopped	6
1/2 cup	chopped onion	125 mL
1/2 cup	chopped celery	125 mL
2 tbsp	all-purpose flour	25 mL
3/4 tsp	salt	4 mL
1/4 tsp	pepper	1 mL
2 cups	chicken stock or water	500 mL
3 cups	diced potatoes	750 mL
2 cups	corn kernels	500 mL
2-1/2 cups	milk	625 mL
2 tbsp	chopped fresh parsley	25 mL

● In large heavy saucepan, cook bacon over medium heat for 4 to 5 minutes or until crisp. Drain off fat.

● Add onion and celery; cook, stirring occasionally, for about 5 minutes or until softened. Sprinkle with flour, salt and pepper; cook, stirring, for 1 minute. Gradually stir in chicken stock until blended.

● Add potatoes; cover and simmer for 10 minutes or until almost tender. Add corn; simmer, covered, for 6 minutes or until vegetables are tender. Stir in milk; bring just to simmer. Ladle into warmed bowls; sprinkle with parsley. Makes 6 servings.

Roasted Tomato and Corn Soup

Roasting deepens the very essence of summer tomatoes.

Per serving: about
- 245 calories
- 9 g fat
- good source of iron
- 9 g protein
- 37 g carbohydrate
- very high source of fiber

2-1/2 lb	plum tomatoes	1.25 kg
1	whole head garlic	1
2	onions, quartered	2
2 tbsp	olive oil	25 mL
1/2 tsp	salt	2 mL
1/4 tsp	pepper	1 mL
1	sweet red pepper	1
2	large corn cobs	2
2-1/2 cups	chicken or vegetable stock	625 mL
2 tbsp	chopped fresh oregano or basil	25 mL
1 tbsp	balsamic or red wine vinegar	15 mL

● Trim stem end of tomatoes; cut in half lengthwise. Place, cut side up, on large foil-lined rimmed baking sheet. Trim 1/2 inch (1 cm) off top of garlic without separating cloves; place on baking sheet along with onions. Lightly brush tomatoes, onion and garlic with oil; sprinkle with half of the salt and the pepper. Add red pepper.

● Roast in 375°F (190°C) oven, turning red pepper occasionally, for about 1 hour and 15 minutes or until tomatoes and red pepper are lightly browned and onions and garlic are very soft. Let cool slightly. Squeeze garlic cloves to remove pulp; discard skins. Peel, core and seed red pepper.

● Meanwhile, in large pot of boiling water, cook corn for about 4 minutes or until tender-crisp. Drain and chill in cold water until cool enough to handle. Using sharp knife, slice kernels off cob; set aside.

● In food processor or blender, in four batches, purée garlic and roasted vegetables, adding 1/2 cup (125 mL) of the chicken stock to each batch. Transfer to saucepan; add remaining chicken stock, corn, oregano, vinegar and remaining salt. Heat until steaming. *(Soup can be cooled in open container in refrigerator. Cover and refrigerate for up to 24 hours; serve reheated or chilled.)* Makes 4 servings.

Cheddar Vegetable Soup ▲

1/3 cup	butter	75 mL
1 cup	each finely chopped carrots and celery	250 mL
1	onion, finely chopped	1
3/4 cup	all-purpose flour	175 mL
4 cups	each milk and chicken stock	1 L
1 lb	old Cheddar cheese, cubed	500 g
	Chopped fresh parsley	

● In large heavy saucepan, melt butter over medium heat; cook carrots, celery and onion, stirring often, for 5 minutes or until softened. Sprinkle with flour; stir until blended.

● Pour in milk and chicken stock; bring to boil, whisking often. Reduce heat to medium-low; cook, stirring often, for 10 to 15 minutes or until thickened. Add cheese; stir until melted. Ladle into warmed bowls; sprinkle with parsley. Makes 10 servings.

*S*tudents at the University of British Columbia warm up on cold, damp days with bowlfuls of this quick-to-make, smooth-as-velvet soup, known on campus as Duchess Soup.

Per serving: about
- 345 calories
- 18 g protein
- 24 g fat
- 15 g carbohydrate
- excellent source of calcium

Basic Vegetable Stock

A *recipe for a good basic vegetable stock is a must in every kitchen. Add mushroom stems, if availible.*

Per 1 cup (250 mL): about
- 15 calories
- trace protein
- 1 g fat
- 1 g carbohydrate

1 tsp	vegetable oil	5 mL
2	carrots	2
2	onions, coarsely chopped	2
1	leek, coarsely chopped	1
1	stalk celery (with leaves), chopped	1
10	stems fresh parsley	10
3	sprigs fresh thyme (or 1/2 tsp/2 mL dried)	3
10	peppercorns, cracked	10
2	bay leaves	2
8 cups	cold water	2 L
1/2 tsp	salt	2 mL

● In stockpot, heat oil over medium heat; cook carrots, onions, leek and celery, stirring often, for 10 minutes or until softened but not colored.

● Add parsley, thyme, peppercorns, bay leaves and water; bring to boil. Skim off foam. Reduce heat to medium; simmer for 40 minutes.

● Strain through fine sieve, gently pressing vegetables to extract liquid. Stir in salt. Makes about 5 cups (1.25 L).

Fresh Pea Soup with Mint

F *or fresh peas, you may have to shop at a farmers' market or grow your own. Thankfully, frozen peas, especially the tiny ones, are harvested while still tender and flavorful.*

Per serving: about
- 125 calories
- 6 g protein
- 4 g fat
- 17 g carbohydrate
- very high source of fiber

1 tbsp	butter	15 mL
2	shallots, chopped (or 1 each onion and clove garlic, chopped)	2
4 cups	fresh or frozen green peas	1 L
2 cups	shredded lettuce (leaf or romaine)	500 mL
3 tbsp	chopped fresh mint	50 mL
Pinch	each salt and pepper	Pinch
3 cups	vegetable or chicken stock	750 mL
1/4 cup	sour cream or plain yogurt	50 mL

● In large heavy saucepan, melt butter over medium heat; cook shallots, stirring, for about 5 minutes or until very soft.

● Stir in peas, lettuce, 2 tbsp (25 mL) of the mint, salt and pepper; cook for 1 minute. Pour in vegetable stock; bring to boil. Reduce heat, cover and simmer for about 10 minutes or until peas are very tender.

● Transfer soup, in batches, to food processor or blender; purée until smooth. Return to saucepan; heat until steaming. Ladle into warmed bowls; spoon dollop of sour cream on top and sprinkle with remaining mint. Makes 6 servings.

RoastedVegetable Stock

3	carrots	3
3	onions	3
3	stalks celery (with leaves)	3
1 cup	sliced mushroom stems or caps	250 mL
3	cloves garlic	3
2 tsp	vegetable oil	10 mL
10	stems fresh parsley	10
1 tsp	crumbled dried mushrooms	5 mL
10	peppercorns, cracked	10
2	bay leaves	2
8 cups	cold water	2 L
1/2 tsp	salt	2 mL

● Cut carrots, onions and celery into chunks; place in roasting pan. Add fresh mushrooms, garlic and oil, stirring to coat vegetables. Roast in 450°F (230°C) oven, stirring halfway through, for 40 minutes or until vegetables are softened and browned at edges.

● Transfer to stockpot. Add parsley, dried mushrooms, peppercorns, bay leaves and all but 1 cup (250 mL) of the water.

● Pour remaining water into roasting pan, stirring with wooden spoon to scrape up any brown bits. Pour into stockpot; bring to boil. Skim off foam. Reduce heat to medium; simmer for 40 minutes.

● Strain through fine sieve, gently pressing vegetables to extract liquid. Stir in salt. Makes about 5 cups (1.25 L).

Roasting darkens and deepens the flavor of stock. Freeze in amounts handy for your favorite soups or stews.

Per 1 cup (250 mL): about
- 20 calories
- 2 g fat
- trace protein
- 1 g carbohydrate

Broccoli Soup

1	bunch broccoli	1
2 tbsp	butter	25 mL
1/4 cup	chopped onion	50 mL
1/4 cup	chopped celery	50 mL
1/4 tsp	curry powder	1 mL
2 cups	chicken or vegetable stock	500 mL
1 cup	10% cream	250 mL
1/2 tsp	salt	2 mL
Pinch	pepper	Pinch

● Separate broccoli into florets; reserve 1/2 cup (125 mL) for garnish. Peel stems and chop coarsely. Set aside.

● In large heavy saucepan, melt butter over medium heat; cook onion, celery and curry powder, stirring occasionally, for about 5 minutes or until softened.

● Add broccoli florets and stalks and chicken stock; bring to boil. Reduce heat, cover and simmer for 10 to 15 minutes or until broccoli is just tender.

● Transfer soup, in batches, to food processor or blender; purée until smooth. Return to saucepan. Add cream, salt and pepper; bring just to simmer. Ladle into warmed bowls; float reserved broccoli florets on top. Makes 4 servings.

Even if you're not a fan of broccoli, you'll enjoy this puréed soup that's brightened with broccoli florets and a whisp of curry.

Per serving: about
- 180 calories
- 8 g protein
- 13 g fat
- 10 g carbohydrate

Montebello Beet Soup ▲

*From Le Château
Montebello overlooking the
Ottawa River comes this
magnificently red,
magnificently flavored soup.*

Per serving: about
• 120 calories
• 4 g fat
• 5 g protein
• 15 g carbohydrate

8	beets (1-1/2 lb/750 g)	8
2	potatoes	2
1 tbsp	olive oil	15 mL
1	onion, chopped	1
1 tsp	medium curry powder or paste	5 mL
6 cups	chicken stock	1.5 L
1 tbsp	liquid honey	15 mL
1/4 tsp	salt	1 mL
1/4 cup	sour cream	50 mL
1/4 cup	finely chopped fresh chives or green onions (optional)	50 mL

● Peel beets and potatoes; cut into
1-1/2-inch (4 cm) cubes.

● In large heavy saucepan, heat oil over
medium heat; cook beets, potatoes, onion
and curry powder, stirring often, for about
8 minutes or until onion is softened.

● Add chicken stock, honey and salt; bring
to boil. Reduce heat to medium-low; cover
and simmer for about 25 minutes or until
vegetables are tender. Transfer, in batches,
to food processor or blender; purée until
smooth.

● Return soup to clean saucepan; heat until
simmering. Ladle into warmed bowls. Dollop
each with sour cream; sprinkle with chives
(if using). Makes 8 servings.

Hearty Beet Soup

1 oz	dried mushrooms	30 g
2 tbsp	vegetable oil	25 mL
2	onions, chopped	2
1	clove garlic, minced	1
6	large beets, peeled and cubed (1-1/2 lb/750 g)	6
2	carrots, diced	2
1	stalk celery, diced	1
Half	small parsley root, diced (optional)	Half
1	potato, peeled and diced	1
1	bay leaf	1
2 cups	shredded cabbage	500 mL
1/2 cup	cooked white kidney beans	125 mL
3 tbsp	white vinegar	50 mL
1-1/2 tsp	salt	7 mL
	Pepper	
	Chopped fresh dill	

● In large measure, soak mushrooms in 3 cups (750 mL) hot water for 30 minutes or until softened. Drain through coffee filter, reserving liquid; chop mushrooms and set aside.

● In large heavy saucepan, heat oil over medium-low heat; cook onions, garlic, beets, carrots, celery, parsley root (if using), potato and mushrooms, stirring often, for 5 minutes or until slightly softened.

● Add bay leaf, mushroom liquid and 4 cups (1 L) water; bring to boil. Reduce heat and simmer for 20 minutes or just until beets are tender. Remove from heat.

● Transfer 3 cups (750 mL) of the beet mixture to blender; purée until smooth. Return to pan. Add cabbage; simmer for 5 minutes or until tender-crisp. Stir in beans, vinegar, salt, and pepper to taste; heat through. Discard bay leaf. Ladle into warmed bowls; sprinkle with dill. Makes 8 servings.

T*his vegetable-rich soup is adapted from Savella Stechishin's recipe in* Traditional Ukrainian Cookery.

Per serving: about
- 110 calories
- 4 g fat
- high source of fiber
- 3 g protein
- 18 g carbohydrate

TIP: If dried mushrooms (porcini or morels are recommended) are not available, cook 2 cups (500 mL) sliced fresh mushrooms with the onions.

Carrot, Leek and Rice Soup

1 tbsp	butter or vegetable oil	15 mL
3 cups	sliced carrots	750 mL
2	leeks (white and light green parts only), chopped	2
2	cloves garlic, minced	2
1/2 tsp	dried thyme	2 mL
1/4 tsp	dried oregano	1 mL
1	bay leaf	1
1/4 cup	parboiled rice	50 mL
4 cups	chicken or vegetable stock	1 L
1 cup	peas (optional)	250 mL

● In large heavy saucepan, melt butter over medium-low heat. Add carrots, leeks, garlic, thyme, oregano and bay leaf; cover and cook, stirring occasionally, for about 8 minutes or until leeks are softened.

● Add rice; cook, stirring, for 2 minutes. Pour in chicken stock; bring to boil. Reduce heat, cover and simmer for about 30 minutes or until rice is tender, adding peas for last 5 minutes (if using). Discard bay leaf. Makes 4 servings.

T*his soup is so simple, so easy to simmer up and so good.*

Per serving: about
- 170 calories
- 5 g fat
- 7 g protein
- 24 g carbohydrate

Sorrel and Spinach Soup

Sorrel is a perennial herb with dark green, spade-shape leaves that add a special tang to soup.

Per serving: about
- 180 calories
- 9 g protein
- 14 g fat
- 4 g carbohydrate
- good source of iron

2 tbsp	butter	25 mL
1-1/2 cups	chopped fresh spinach	375 mL
1/2 cup	chopped fresh sorrel	125 mL
4 cups	chicken stock	1 L
3	egg yolks	3
1/2 cup	10% cream	125 mL
1/4 tsp	pepper	1 mL
2 tbsp	chopped fresh parsley or chervil	25 mL

● In large heavy saucepan, melt butter over medium heat; cook spinach and sorrel, stirring, for about 1 minute or until wilted. Pour in chicken stock; bring to boil. Reduce heat and simmer for 3 minutes.

● In small bowl, whisk egg yolks with cream; stir in about 1/2 cup (125 mL) of the hot stock mixture. Gradually stir egg mixture back into pan; cook over medium heat, stirring constantly, for 3 to 5 minutes or until slightly thickened. Season with pepper. Ladle into warmed bowls; sprinkle with parsley. Makes 4 servings.

TIP: If sorrel isn't available, substitute additional spinach. Substitute chopped fresh dill for the parsley, adding half with the egg yolks and using remainder as garnish.

Herbed Tomato Soup

Canned tomatoes are one of the handiest ingredients in a cupboard — handy for pasta sauces, for stews and for this pleasing soup.

Per serving: about
- 125 calories
- 6 g protein
- 5 g fat
- 17 g carbohydrate
- good source of iron

1 tbsp	butter	15 mL
1	large clove garlic, minced	1
1	large onion, chopped	1
1/2 tsp	each dried basil and thyme	2 mL
1/4 tsp	each crumbled dried rosemary and pepper	1 mL
4 tsp	all-purpose flour	20 mL
1	can (28 oz/796 mL) tomatoes, chopped	1
3 cups	chicken stock	750 mL
1/2 tsp	granulated sugar	2 mL

● In large heavy saucepan, melt butter over medium heat; cook garlic, onion, basil, thyme, rosemary and pepper, stirring occasionally, for about 4 minutes or until onion is softened. Sprinkle with flour; cook, stirring, for 2 minutes.

● Stir in tomatoes, chicken stock and sugar; bring to boil. Reduce heat and simmer for 45 minutes. Transfer soup, in batches, to food processor or blender; purée until smooth. Makes 4 servings.

VARIATION
● TOMATO MUSHROOM SOUP: Add 1-1/2 cups (375 mL) sliced mushrooms along with onion; cook for 8 minutes or until liquid is evaporated and mushrooms just start to turn golden. Do not purée.

Mexican Gazpacho with Avocado Salsa

3	ripe tomatoes (about 1 lb/500 g)	3
1	English cucumber (about 1 lb/500 g)	1
1	each sweet green and red pepper, coarsely chopped	1
2	cloves garlic, minced	2
2 tbsp	lime juice	25 mL
1 tbsp	olive oil	15 mL
1/4 tsp	jalapeño sauce or hot pepper sauce	1 mL
3 cups	tomato juice	750 mL
2 tbsp	chopped fresh coriander	25 mL
1/4 tsp	each salt and pepper	1 mL
	AVOCADO SALSA	
2	ripe avocados, peeled and chopped	2
2 tbsp	chopped fresh coriander	25 mL
2 tbsp	lime juice	25 mL
1/4 tsp	salt	1 mL

● With paring knife, score X on bottom skin of each tomato. Plunge tomatoes into pot of boiling water for 30 seconds. Remove and chill briefly in cold water; drain and peel off skins.

Don't even think of making gazpacho when tomatoes are out of season. Since the success of the soup depends mainly on fully sun-ripened tomatoes, it's worth the wait for local or homegrown.

● Cut tomatoes in half; scoop out seeds. Chop tomatoes; set 1 cup (250 mL) aside. Peel and chop cucumber; set 1-1/2 cups (375 mL) aside.

● In batches in food processor or blender, purée tomatoes, cucumber, green and red peppers, garlic, lime juice, oil and jalapeño sauce until smooth.

● Transfer to large bowl; stir in tomato juice, coriander, salt, pepper and reserved tomatoes and cucumbers. Cover and refrigerate for at least 2 hours or until chilled. *(Soup can be refrigerated for up to 12 hours.)*

● AVOCADO SALSA: In small bowl, combine avocado, coriander, lime juice and salt. Ladle gazpacho into chilled bowls; top with salsa. Makes 6 servings.

The earthy flavor of coriander, the nip of jalapeño and the smooth texture of avocado set off a summery tomato, cucumber and sweet pepper gazpacho.

Per serving: about
- 185 calories
- 13 g fat
- good source of iron
- 4 g protein
- 18 g carbohydrate
- high source of fiber

Golden Gazpacho

Stray from the classic gazpacho and savor a smoky sweet pepper and peach version.

Per serving: about
- 85 calories
- trace fat
- 2 g protein
- 21 g carbohydrate

2	sweet yellow peppers	2
1	sweet red pepper	1
4	peaches, peeled and pitted	4
1	clove garlic, minced	1
1/2 cup	peach nectar	125 mL
1/2 cup	vegetable stock	125 mL
2 tbsp	chopped fresh chives	25 mL
1 tbsp	white wine vinegar	15 mL
1/4 tsp	each salt and pepper	1 mL
Dash	hot pepper sauce	Dash

● Place yellow and red peppers on greased grill or rimmed baking sheet; cook over medium-high heat or broil, turning often, for about 20 minutes or until charred. Let cool slightly; peel and seed, reserving any juices in large bowl.

● In food processor or blender, purée half of the peppers and half of the peaches until smooth; add to juices in bowl.

● Cut remaining peppers and peaches into small chunks. Add to bowl along with garlic, peach nectar, vegetable stock, 1 tbsp (15 mL) of the chives, vinegar, salt, pepper and hot pepper sauce. Cover and refrigerate for about 1 hour or until chilled. *(Soup can be refrigerated for up to 4 hours.)* Ladle into chilled bowls; sprinkle with remaining chives. Makes 4 servings.

TIP: Nectarines can replace the peaches. No matter which of these luscious summer fruits you use, make sure they are in-season ripe, juicy and fragrant.

Iced Cucumber and Yogurt Soup

Not only is this appetizer soup cold but it's also served over ice cubes that melt and form part of the broth.

Per serving: about
- 200 calories
- 14 g fat
- good source of calcium
- 8 g protein
- 12 g carbohydrate

Half	English cucumber (or 4 dill-size field cucumbers)	Half
3/4 tsp	salt	4 mL
1/2 cup	walnut halves	125 mL
2 cups	plain yogurt	500 mL
1 tbsp	finely chopped fresh dill	15 mL
1	small clove garlic, minced	1
1 tbsp	extra virgin olive oil	15 mL
1 cup	crushed ice	250 mL
	Fresh dill sprigs	

● Peel cucumber. (If using field cucumbers, cut in half lengthwise and scoop out seeds.) Cut into 1/4-inch (5 mm) dice to make about 1 cup (250 mL). Toss with salt; let drain in colander for 30 minutes. Rinse and pat thoroughly dry on towels. *(Cucumber can be prepared to this point, enclosed in towel, then plastic bag and refrigerated for up to 4 hours.)*

● Reserving four of the best walnut halves for garnish, chop remaining walnuts finely; set aside.

● In large bowl, whisk together yogurt, chopped dill, garlic and oil; stir in cucumber and chopped walnuts. Divide ice among chilled bowls; ladle soup over top. Garnish each with dill sprigs and walnut half. Makes 4 servings.

TIP: Shop for walnuts labelled California in a store with a high turnover. With most other shelled walnuts, there is a risk of rancidity — and even one rancid walnut can spoil a dish.

Frosty Cucumber Soup with Garnishes

1-1/2	English cucumbers (or 3 field cucumbers)	1-1/2
3 cups	chilled chicken stock	750 mL
3 cups	light sour cream	750 mL
1	clove garlic, minced	1
3 tbsp	white wine vinegar	50 mL
1 tsp	salt	5 mL
	GARNISH	
1-1/2 cups	chopped tomatoes	375 mL
3/4 cup	sliced almonds, toasted	175 mL
1/2 cup	sliced green onions	125 mL
1/2 cup	finely chopped fresh parsley (preferably Italian)	125 mL
1/2 cup	finely chopped sweet red or green pepper	125 mL

● Peel cucumbers. (If using field cucumbers, cut in half lengthwise; scoop out seeds.) Cut into coarse cubes to make about 3 cups (750 mL).

● In food processor or blender, purée cucumber with 1 cup (250 mL) of the chicken stock; transfer to large bowl. Stir in remaining chicken stock. Whisk in sour cream, garlic, vinegar and salt. Refrigerate for about 1 hour or until chilled.

● GARNISH: Place tomatoes, almonds, green onions, parsley and red pepper in separate small bowls. Ladle soup into chilled bowls; let guests choose garnishes to sprinkle over top. Makes 8 servings.

Mix and match to your heart and tummy's content with a creamy cucumber soup topped with your choice of tomatoes, toasted almonds, green onions and sweet peppers.

Per serving: about
● 225 calories
● 18 g fat
● 7 g protein
● 11 g carbohydrate

TIPS

● If you wish, just coarsely grate the cucumbers and omit the puréeing.

● To toast almonds, place on rimmed baking sheet in center of 350°F (180°C) oven and toast for 5 to 10 minutes or until fragrant; let cool.

Smooth Watercress Soup

1 tbsp	butter	15 mL
2	leeks (white and light green parts only), sliced	2
3 cups	chicken stock	750 mL
2	large potatoes, peeled and cubed	2
1	bunch watercress	1
1 cup	milk or 18% cream	250 mL
	Salt and pepper	

● In large heavy saucepan, melt butter over medium heat; cook leeks, covered and stirring occasionally, for 10 minutes or until softened, adding up to 2 tbsp (25 mL) of the chicken stock if mixture seems dry.

● Add potatoes and remaining chicken stock; bring to boil. Reduce heat to medium; simmer for 20 minutes.

● Reserve 1/2 cup (125 mL) of the watercress leaves. Add remaining watercress to saucepan; cook for 1 minute or just until wilted.

● Transfer soup, in batches, to food processor or blender; purée until smooth. Blend in milk. Refrigerate for about 4 hours or until chilled. *(Soup can be refrigerated for up to 8 hours.)* Season with salt and pepper to taste. Chop reserved watercress. Ladle soup into chilled bowls; sprinkle with watercress. Makes 4 servings.

A soup that's cool and summery is perfection for warm-weather entertaining.

Per serving: about
● 185 calories
● 5 g fat
● 8 g protein
● 26 g carbohydrate

Strawberry Melon Soup with Mint ▲

If you've never tried a fruit soup, this passionately pink and melon-fragrant blend should be your first. We guarantee it won't be your last.

Per serving: about
- 90 calories
- trace fat
- 1 g protein
- 18 g carbohydrate

4-1/2 cups	cubed peeled cantaloupe (about 3 lb/1.5 kg)	1.125 L
3/4 cup	strawberries, hulled	175 mL
3 tbsp	granulated sugar	50 mL
1-1/4 cups	orange juice	300 mL
3/4 cup	fruity white wine	175 mL
3 tbsp	lemon juice	50 mL
2 tbsp	finely chopped fresh spearmint	25 mL

● In food processor or blender, purée cantaloupe with strawberries until smooth; pour into bowl. Add sugar; stir until dissolved.

● Stir in orange juice, wine and lemon juice. Cover and refrigerate for about 2 hours or until chilled. *(Soup can be refrigerated for up to 24 hours.)* Stir in spearmint just before serving. Makes 8 servings.

TIP: Spearmint's taste is the best for this fruit combo. Other popular garden mints, such as lemon balm, orange, apple or pineapple mint and peppermint, will overpower the subtleties of strawberries and melon.

Black Cherry and Wine Soup

1-1/2 cups	fruity dry white wine (preferably Riesling)	375 mL
1/4 cup	granulated sugar	50 mL
3	strips (1/2-inch/1 cm wide) lemon peel	3
1/4 cup	lemon juice	50 mL
Half	stick cinnamon	Half
2	whole cloves	2
2 cups	pitted black cherries (12 oz/375 g)	500 mL
1 cup	light sour cream	250 mL
1/4 cup	10% cream	50 mL

● In large heavy saucepan, combine wine, sugar, lemon peel, lemon juice, cinnamon and cloves; bring to boil. Add cherries; return to boil. Reduce heat and simmer for about 5 minutes or until cherries are barely tender. Let cool. Discard cinnamon, cloves and lemon peel.

● Transfer soup, in batches, to food processor or blender; purée until smooth. Transfer to bowl; blend in sour cream and 10% cream. Refrigerate for about 4 hours or until chilled. Makes 8 servings.

Lightened up but still luxurious, this vividly pink soup is a treat when cherries are at their most perfumed and the occasion is most special.

Per serving: about
- 115 calories
- 3 g protein
- 3 g fat
- 17 g carbohydrate

Chilly Cauliflower Vichyssoise

2 tsp	butter	10 mL
1	leek (white part only), chopped	1
1	clove garlic, minced	1
Pinch	nutmeg	Pinch
1	bay leaf	1
1-1/2 cups	chicken stock	375 mL
4 cups	cauliflower florets (about half a head)	1 L
1	small potato, peeled and cubed	1
1 cup	milk	250 mL
1/4 tsp	each salt and white pepper	1 mL
1/4 cup	chopped fresh chives	50 mL

● In large heavy saucepan, melt butter over medium heat; cook leek, garlic, nutmeg and bay leaf, stirring occasionally, for 4 minutes or until leek is softened but not colored.

● Add chicken stock; bring to boil. Add cauliflower and potato. Reduce heat to medium; cover and simmer for 15 minutes or until vegetables are very tender. Discard bay leaf.

● Transfer soup, in batches, to food processor or blender; purée until smooth. Transfer to large bowl. Whisk in milk, salt and pepper. Refrigerate for about 4 hours or until chilled. *(Soup can be refrigerated for up to 12 hours.)* Ladle into chilled bowls; sprinkle with chives. Makes 6 servings.

Add cauliflower to this French favorite and you still have the creamy cool color plus a boost of delicate cauliflower flavor.

Per serving: about
- 80 calories
- 4 g protein
- 3 g fat
- 10 g carbohydrate

ICE BOWLS

Food stylist Ruth Gangbar shares her technique for making ice bowls that are perfect for chilled soups (photo, p. 30).

● For each ice bowl, you need two cereal or soup bowls — a small one, and a larger one that's about 3/4 inch (2 cm) deeper and wider.

● Using duct or electrical tape, secure top of smaller bowl to top of large bowl, keeping smaller bowl suspended. Place bowls on level rimmed baking sheet.

● Fill space between bowls about three-quarters full with distilled water or tap water that has stood overnight at room temperature.

● Add flower petals or other edible decorative items to water. Place level in freezer; freeze until solid.

Asian Shrimp and Noodle Soup ▶

This is Asian-style supper in a bowl.

Per serving: about
- 230 calories
- 7 g fat
- good source of iron
- 19 g protein
- 22 g carbohydrate

1 tsp	vegetable oil	5 mL
3	green onions, thinly sliced diagonally	3
2	cloves garlic, minced	2
4	slices peeled gingerroot	4
6	fresh shiitake mushrooms, stemmed and sliced	6
1/2 cup	thinly sliced bamboo shoots	125 mL
5 cups	chicken stock	1.25 L
3 tbsp	rice vinegar	50 mL
2 tsp	sesame oil	10 mL
2 cups	broad egg noodles (about 3 oz/90 g)	500 mL
8 oz	raw large shrimp, peeled and deveined	250 g
4 oz	snow peas, cut in half, or pea shoots	125 g

● In large heavy saucepan, heat vegetable oil over medium heat; cook onions, garlic, ginger, mushrooms and bamboo shoots, stirring, for 2 minutes.

● Pour in chicken stock, vinegar and sesame oil; bring to boil, skimming off any foam. Reduce heat and simmer for 5 minutes.

● Add noodles; cover and cook for about 10 minutes or until noodles are tender. Add shrimp and snow peas; cook, covered, for 3 minutes or until shrimp are bright pink and snow peas are tender. Makes 4 servings.

VARIATION
● ASIAN SALMON NOODLE SOUP: Substitute thinly sliced water chestnuts for the bamboo shoots, and boneless fresh salmon chunks for the shrimp. Substitute fine egg noodles, or rice or wheat vermicelli noodles for the broad egg noodles.

Thai Shrimp Soup

Tom Yum Goong is usually hot enough to make you whimper with pleasure but we've tamed the heat so you can enjoy the other flavors in this popular Thai soup — lemon, ginger, lemongrass and shrimp.

Per serving: about
- 110 calories
- 2 g fat
- good source of iron
- 15 g protein
- 9 g carbohydrate

1	stalk lemongrass	1
1	can (10 oz/284 mL) chicken broth	1
2 tbsp	lime juice	25 mL
8	thin slices gingerroot	8
2 tbsp	lemon juice	25 mL
1 tbsp	fish sauce	15 mL
1 tsp	Asian chili paste	5 mL
3 cups	sliced mushrooms (8 oz/250 g)	750 mL
8 oz	raw shrimp, peeled and deveined	250 g
1 cup	snow peas, trimmed	250 mL
1	green or red chili, sliced	1

● Trim lemongrass; cut into 2-inch (5 cm) lengths and crush with meat pounder.

● In large heavy saucepan, combine lemongrass, 5 cups (1.25 L) water, chicken broth, lime juice and ginger; bring to boil and boil for 5 minutes. Reduce heat to low. Stir in lemon juice, fish sauce and chili paste; simmer for 2 minutes.

● Add mushrooms and shrimp; cook for 2 to 3 minutes or until shrimp are barely firm. Add snow peas and green chili; cook for 1 minute or until snow peas are bright green. Makes 4 servings.

VARIATION
● HOT THAI SOUP WITH SALMON OR SCALLOPS: Omit shrimp. Substitute 6 oz (175 g) salmon or scallops sliced thinly across the grain.

TIPS
● You can substitute 2 long strips of lemon rind for lemongrass.
● If you have you own homemade chicken stock, you can substitute it for the canned broth and water.

HOT SUBSTITUTIONS

● While fresh chilies, hot pepper sauce, hot pepper flakes (also known as red pepper flakes or chili flakes), Asian chili sauce or chili oil, Portuguese piri piri, sambal oelek and cayenne pepper all provide different flavors and even varying degrees of heat, in a pinch they can be substituted for each other.

● Use common sense and add to the dish prudently, knowing you can always stir in more, whereas it's almost impossible to tame the fire. For hot fiends, there is always the option of providing a bottle of hot sauce or shaker of hot pepper flakes at the table to satisfy their appetite for hot licks.

Hot-and-Sour Shrimp Soup

D*on't let the long list of ingredients deter you; this popular soup is really easy and quick to make.*

Per serving: about
- 175 calories
- 18 g protein
- 6 g fat
- 12 g carbohydrate
- good source of iron

6 cups	chicken stock	1.5 L	8 oz	raw medium shrimp, peeled and deveined		250 g
2	small onions, slivered	2	4 oz	tofu		125 g
2-1/2 cups	sliced mushrooms (about 8 oz/250 g)	625 mL	3 tbsp	cornstarch		50 mL
3 tbsp	soy sauce	50 mL	2	eggs, lightly beaten		2
3 tbsp	rice vinegar	50 mL	1/4 cup	chopped fresh chives or green onions		50 mL
2 tbsp	Worcestershire sauce	25 mL				
1 tbsp	minced gingerroot	15 mL				
1	clove garlic, minced	1				
1 tsp	sesame oil	5 mL				
1/2 tsp	pepper	2 mL				
1/4 tsp	hot pepper flakes	1 mL				

● In large heavy saucepan, bring chicken stock, onions and mushrooms to boil; reduce heat and simmer for 10 minutes. Add soy sauce, vinegar, Worcestershire sauce, ginger, garlic, oil, pepper and hot pepper flakes; simmer for 5 minutes. *(Soup can be prepared to this point, cooled in refrigerator, covered and stored for up to 12 hours. Reheat to steaming.)*

● Meanwhile, cut shrimp in half lengthwise. Cut tofu into thin strips. Add shrimp and tofu to soup; simmer for 3 minutes. Stir 1/3 cup (75 mL) water with cornstarch until mixture is smooth; stir into soup and cook over low heat, stirring often, for about 5 minutes or until thickened.

● Remove from heat; drizzle in eggs, whisking with fork to form streamers. Ladle into warmed bowls; sprinkle with chives. Makes 6 servings.

Chunky Lobster Chowder

3 tbsp	butter	50 mL
1/2 cup	chopped green onions	125 mL
1-1/4 tsp	salt	6 mL
1 tsp	dried thyme	5 mL
1/4 tsp	pepper	1 mL
1/4 cup	all-purpose flour	50 mL
3 cups	cubed red-skinned potatoes	750 mL
1-1/2 cups	corn kernels	375 mL
1	can (11.3 oz/320 g) frozen lobster meat	1
2-1/2 cups	milk	625 mL
1/2 cup	10% cream	125 mL
1 tbsp	chopped fresh dill	15 mL

● In large heavy saucepan, melt butter over medium heat; cook green onions, salt, thyme and pepper, stirring occasionally, for about 4 minutes or until softened. Sprinkle with flour; cook, stirring, for 1 minute. Whisk in 1 cup (250 mL) water.

● Add potatoes; bring to boil. Reduce heat to low, cover and simmer for about 8 minutes or until potatoes are tender. Add corn and lobster; cook, covered, for 5 minutes. Gradually stir in milk, cream and dill; heat through. Makes 6 servings.

W hen new potatoes and corn have been harvested and lobster is in season, simmer a pot of this quintessential summer soup. Frozen canned lobster meat makes this luxurious soup easy to make — no picking the meat out of claw and tail — and more available inland.

Per serving: about
● 280 calories   ● 18 g protein
● 10 g fat   ● 30 g carbohydrate
● good source
  of calcium

TIPS
● If desired, substitute 2 cups (500 mL) cubed uncooked salmon or medium shrimp for the lobster.
● You can use chopped fresh basil or coriander instead of the dill.

Newfoundland Cod Chowder

4	strips bacon	4
2	onions, sliced	2
1 tsp	dried savory	5 mL
6	potatoes, peeled and cubed	6
3	carrots, sliced	3
1 tsp	salt	5 mL
1-1/2 lb	fresh cod fillets	750 g
1	can (385 mL) evaporated milk	1
1/4 tsp	pepper	1 mL
2 tbsp	chopped fresh parsley or chives	25 mL

● In large heavy saucepan, cook bacon over medium-high heat for about 10 minutes or until crisp; drain on paper towel. Crumble and set aside.

● Drain off all but 1 tbsp (15 mL) fat from pan. Add onions and savory; cook, stirring occasionally, for 5 minutes or until softened.

● Add potatoes, carrots, 4 cups (1 L) water and salt; bring to boil. Cover, reduce heat and simmer for about 20 minutes or just until vegetables are tender.

● Cut cod into 1-inch (2.5 cm) chunks; add to pan and simmer for 5 minutes. Add milk and pepper; heat until steaming and fish flakes easily when tested with fork. Ladle into warmed bowls; sprinkle with bacon and parsley. Makes 8 servings.

A chowder made with fresh North Atlantic cod is thick and scrumptious, especially served Newfoundland-style with thick slices of homemade bread.

Per serving: about
● 260 calories   ● 22 g protein
● 5 g fat   ● 31 g carbohydrate
● good source
  of calcium

TIP: You can replace bacon and bacon fat with 1 tbsp (15 mL) unsalted butter or vegetable oil. Garnish with seasoned croutons.

PEI Oyster Chowder ◄

8	oysters	8
1 tbsp	butter	15 mL
1	each stalk celery and small onion, diced	1
6	fennel seeds, crushed	6
1 cup	fish or chicken stock	250 mL
1	russet potato, peeled and finely cubed	1
1/3 cup	whipping cream	75 mL
1/4 tsp	pepper	1 mL

● Shuck oysters; reserve liquor. In heavy saucepan, melt butter over medium-low heat; cook celery, onion and fennel seeds, stirring often, for 10 minutes or until onion is translucent.

● Add fish stock and potato; cook over medium heat, stirring occasionally, for 10 minutes or until tender. Add cream; simmer for 2 to 3 minutes or until hot. Do not boil. Add oysters, liquor and pepper. Makes 2 servings.

Chef Stefan Czapalay of Seasons in Thyme Restaurant in Tyne Valley, PEI, serves this oyster chowder using Malpeque oysters harvested nearby.

Per serving: about
- 315 calories
- 9 g protein
- 22 g fat
- 21 g carbohydrate
- excellent source of iron

Newfoundland Mussels

3 lb	mussels	1.5 kg
1 cup	white wine	250 mL
2	shallots, finely chopped	2
Pinch	saffron	Pinch
1/4 tsp	salt	1 mL
2 tbsp	chopped fresh chives	25 mL

● Scrub mussels under running water and remove any beards; discard any that do not close when tapped.

● In large heavy saucepan, bring wine, shallots, saffron and salt to boil; reduce heat to medium. Add mussels; cover and cook for 4 to 6 minutes or until mussels open. Discard any that do not open.

● With slotted spoon, transfer mussels to bowls; spoon liquid over top. Garnish with chives. Makes 4 servings.

Per serving: about • 115 calories • 12 g protein • 2 g fat • 5 g carbohydrate • excellent source of iron

Soup or stew? Sometimes the two categories come together, as they do in this flavorful bowlful of mussels created by Steven Watson, executive chef of the Hotel Newfoundland in St. John's.

OYSTERS FOR CHOWDERS

● Already shucked oysters are available fresh or frozen and are a great convenience when making soups and chowders. They should smell fresh and be packed in clear, not cloudy, oyster liquor.

● When starting out with oysters live in the shell, look for tightly closed and undamaged shells; if gaping slightly, shells should close when tapped.

SHUCKING OYSTERS

1 Scrub oysters with brush under cold running water.

2 Protecting hand with folded towel or oven mitt, hold oyster in palm, with cup or deep side down. Brace hand on work surface and keep bottom shell level to prevent spilling liquor.

3 Insert oyster knife between shells, gently working back and forth close to hinge at pointed end. Twist up and down, back and forth to open shell.

4 Slide knife across top of shell to cut muscle. Discard top shell, then run knife under oyster meat.

Egg and Lemon Soup

In avgolemono, the Greek lemon, broth and orzo soup, eggs are the thickening and enriching agent.

Per serving: about
- 155 calories
- 13 g protein
- 6 g fat
- 12 g carbohydrate

6 cups	chicken stock	1.5 L
1/3 cup	orzo or small pasta	75 mL
4	eggs	4
3 tbsp	lemon juice	50 mL
1	lemon, thinly sliced	1
1/4 cup	chopped fresh parsley	50 mL

● In large heavy saucepan, bring chicken stock to boil. Stir in orzo; cook for 6 to 8 minutes or until tender but firm. Reduce heat to medium-low.

● Meanwhile, in bowl, whisk eggs for about 1 minute or until pale and frothy; slowly whisk in lemon juice. Whisking constantly, gradually add 1 cup (250 mL) of the hot stock; whisk back into pan in slow steady stream (will be very frothy).

● Cook over medium-low heat, stirring constantly with wooden spoon, for 10 to 12 minutes or until thick enough to coat back of spoon; immediately remove from heat. Ladle into warmed bowls; top with lemon slice and sprinkle with parsley. Makes 5 servings.

Homemade Chicken Soup ▶

The real thing — chicken soup that begins with a chicken, herbs and flavorful vegetables — puts other chicken soups to shame.

Per serving: about
- 185 calories
- 16 g protein
- 7 g fat
- 13 g carbohydrate

2 tbsp	butter	25 mL
1/2 cup	minced onion	125 mL
1-1/2 cups	sliced carrots	375 mL
1-1/2 cups	sliced celery	375 mL
1 cup	sliced parsnips	250 mL
1-1/2 cups	egg noodles	375 mL
1/4 cup	chopped fresh parsley	50 mL
	Hot pepper sauce	
	Salt and pepper	
	HOMEMADE CHICKEN STOCK	
1	stewing hen or roasting chicken (5 lb/2.2 kg)	1
2	carrots, chopped	2
2	stalks celery, chopped	2
1	onion, chopped	1
1	leek, chopped (optional)	1
3	sprigs fresh parsley	3
1	bay leaf	1
1 tsp	salt	5 mL
1/2 tsp	dried thyme	2 mL
1/2 tsp	whole black peppercorns	2 mL

● HOMEMADE CHICKEN STOCK: In large stockpot or Dutch oven, bring chicken and 16 cups (4 L) water to boil; skim off foam. Add carrots, celery, onion, leek (if using), parsley, bay leaf, salt, thyme and peppercorns; reduce heat and simmer, partially covered, for 2 to 2-1/2 hours for hen, 1 to 1-1/2 hours for chicken, or until meat can easily be removed from bones.

● Remove chicken from pot and refrigerate. Strain liquid through cheesecloth-lined sieve into large bowl, pressing vegetables to extract as much liquid as possible. Discard vegetables; let stock cool. Refrigerate for at least 8 hours or until fat congeals on surface.

● With slotted spoon, remove fat and discard. Set 8 cups (2 L) stock aside. *(Remaining 7 cups/1.75 L stock can be refrigerated in airtight container for up to 3 days or frozen for up to 4 months.)*

● In large heavy saucepan, melt butter over medium heat; cook onion, stirring occasionally, for 3 minutes or until softened. Add reserved 8 cups (2 L) chicken stock; bring to boil. Add carrots, celery and parsnips; cover and cook over medium-high heat for 5 minutes. Add noodles; cook, uncovered, for 8 to 10 minutes or until noodles and vegetables are tender.

● Meanwhile, remove skin and bones from cooked chicken. Dice 2 cups (500 mL) meat for soup; refrigerate remaining chicken for another use. Add chicken, parsley, and hot pepper sauce, salt and pepper to taste to soup; cook until steaming. Makes 8 servings.

VARIATION

● ASIAN CHICKEN SOUP: Add 1 tbsp (15 mL) chopped gingerroot to onions while softening. Reduce carrots and celery to 1 cup (250 mL) each, diagonally sliced. Substitute 1 cup (250 mL) diagonally sliced bok choy for the parsnips. Omit egg noodles and cook soup for 10 to 15 minutes or until vegetables are softened. Add 1 cup (250 mL) snow peas, 1/4 cup (50 mL) sherry and 2 tbsp (25 mL) soy sauce along with the chicken. Omit parsley and hot pepper sauce.

Smoky Sausage and Chick-Pea Soup ▼

Hearty, with a touch of spice, this soup keeps in the fridge for two days. It's ideal for reheating after a curling match or a stint of cross-country skiing.

Per serving: about
- 240 calories
- 12 g fat
- good source of iron
- 15 g protein
- 21 g carbohydrate
- high source of fiber

1 lb	fresh turkey sausage	500 g
1 tsp	vegetable oil	5 mL
1	onion, chopped	1
4	cloves garlic, minced	4
1	large carrot, chopped	1
1	stalk celery, chopped	1
2	jalapeño peppers, thinly sliced	2
1 tsp	ground cumin	5 mL
1/2 tsp	each ground coriander and paprika	2 mL
1/4 tsp	each chili powder and pepper	1 mL
1	can (19 oz/540 mL) tomatoes	1
1	can (19 oz/540 mL) chick-peas, drained and rinsed	1
3 cups	chicken stock	750 mL
1/4 cup	chopped fresh coriander or parsley	50 mL
1	avocado	1
2	limes	2

● Remove casings from sausage; cut into slices. In large heavy saucepan, heat oil over medium heat; cook sausage, without stirring, for 5 minutes. Add onion, garlic, carrot and celery; cook, stirring often, for about 10 minutes or until vegetables are softened and sausage is cooked through. Drain off any fat.

● Stir in jalapeño peppers, cumin, ground coriander, paprika, chili powder and pepper; cook, stirring, for 1 minute. Add tomatoes, breaking up into small pieces with spoon; bring to boil. Reduce heat, cover and simmer for 10 minutes.

● Add chick-peas, chicken stock and 2 tbsp (25 mL) of the fresh coriander; cover and simmer for 20 minutes. *(Soup can be cooled and refrigerated in airtight container for up to 2 days; reheat gently, adding up to 1/3 cup/75 mL more stock if too thick.)*

● Meanwhile, halve avocado and remove pit. To dice, cut through flesh to skin lengthwise and crosswise; with spoon, scoop out cubes into bowl. Squeeze juice from 1 of the limes; toss juice with avocado. Slice remaining lime into 8 wedges.

● Ladle soup into warmed bowls; garnish with avocado and lime wedge. Sprinkle with remaining coriander. Makes 8 servings.

TIPS

● Mild Italian sausage or fresh chorizo can replace the turkey sausage; omit the paprika.

● If you don't have jalapeño peppers, substitute 1/4 tsp (1 mL) cayenne pepper or hot pepper flakes.

Cock-a-Leekie Soup

2 tbsp	vegetable oil	25 mL
2 cups	sliced leeks	500 mL
2	boneless skinless chicken breasts, cubed	2
6 cups	chicken stock	1.5 L
3/4 cup	long grain rice	175 mL
1	strip lemon peel (2 inches/5 cm long)	1
1	bay leaf	1
1 tsp	salt	5 mL
1/4 tsp	pepper	1 mL
2 tbsp	chopped fresh parsley	25 mL

● In large heavy saucepan, heat oil over medium heat; cook leeks, covered and stirring occasionally, for about 5 minutes or until softened.

● Add chicken; cook over medium-high heat, stirring, for about 4 minutes or until no longer pink inside.

● Add chicken stock, rice, lemon peel and bay leaf; bring to boil. Reduce heat and simmer for about 20 minutes or until rice is tender. Discard lemon peel and bay leaf. Season with salt and pepper. Ladle into warmed bowls; sprinkle with parsley. Makes 4 servings.

You can let winter winds blow if you have a steaming bowl of this chunky chicken soup to ward off the shivers.

Per serving: about
- 320 calories
- 24 g protein
- 10 g fat
- 31 g carbohydrate

Mulligatawny Turkey Soup

2 tsp	vegetable oil	10 mL
4	cloves garlic, minced	4
2 tsp	ground ginger	10 mL
1 tsp	curry powder	5 mL
1/2 tsp	cinnamon	2 mL
1	potato, peeled and chopped	1
1	apple, peeled and chopped	1
3 cups	turkey or chicken stock	750 mL
2 cups	fresh or frozen chopped mixed vegetables	500 mL
2 cups	diced cooked turkey	500 mL
1/2 tsp	salt	2 mL
2 tbsp	chopped fresh coriander or parsley	25 mL

● In large heavy saucepan, heat oil over medium heat; cook garlic, ginger, curry powder and cinnamon, stirring, for 1 minute.

● Add potato, apple, turkey stock and vegetables; cover and simmer for 20 minutes or until vegetables are tender.

● Transfer soup, in batches, to food processor or blender; purée until smooth. Return to pan. Add turkey and salt; cook until steaming. Ladle into warmed bowls; sprinkle with coriander. Makes 6 servings.

When you're looking for ways to use up leftover holiday turkey, stop at soup. Here, a mild version of an Indian soup is delicious topped with a dollop of yogurt and fresh apple slices.

Per serving: about
- 170 calories
- 18 g protein
- 5 g fat
- 13 g carbohydrate

Tomato Turkey Stock

Here's how to make a superior turkey stock, one that will have you waiting for the next occasion to serve turkey. Use it as the base for delicious post-holiday soups.

Per 1 cup (250 mL): about
• 50 calories   • 5 g protein
• 1 g fat   • 4 g carbohydrate

1	turkey carcass	1
1	onion, chopped	1
2	carrots, chopped	2
1	bay leaf	1
10	peppercorns	10
1/4 cup	parsley stalks	50 mL
1	can (10 oz/284 mL) chicken broth	1
1	can (19 oz/540 mL) tomatoes	1

● Break up turkey carcass into quarters. In stockpot, combine carcass, onion, carrots, bay leaf, peppercorns, parsley, 8 cups (2 L) water, chicken broth and tomatoes; bring to boil. Skim off foam.

● Reduce heat and simmer for 2-1/2 hours. Remove and discard carcass. Strain stock through cheesecloth-lined sieve into large bowl, pressing vegetables to extract as much liquid as possible. Let cool.

● Cover and refrigerate for at least 8 hours or until fat congeals on surface. With slotted spoon, remove fat and discard. Makes about 7 cups (1.75 L).

Handy Homemade Chicken Stock

Save on expensive canned chicken stock by making your own. Homemade stock also lets you control the amount of salt in a dish. Freeze in amounts to suit your recipes.

Per 1 cup (250 mL): about
• 40 calories   • 5 g protein
• 1 g fat   • 1 g carbohydrate

3 lb	chicken backs and necks	1.5 kg
1	onion	1
4	whole cloves	4
4	springs fresh parsley	4
1	each stalk celery and carrot, chopped	1
1 tsp	dried thyme	5 mL
1	bay leaf	1

● In stockpot, combine 12 cups (3 L) water, chicken parts, onion, cloves, parsley, celery, carrot, thyme and bay leaf; bring to boil. Skim off foam.

● Reduce heat and simmer for 1-1/2 hours. Strain through cheesecloth-lined sieve into large bowl, pressing vegetables to extract as much liquid as possible. Let cool.

● Cover and refrigerate for at least 8 hours or until fat congeals on surface. With slotted spoon, remove fat and discard. Makes about 8-1/2 cups (2.125 L).

With homemade chicken stock in the freezer, a bowlful of soothing chicken soup is only a simmer away.

Lentil Potato Soup with Bacon

3	strips bacon, chopped	3
1	onion, chopped	1
1	clove garlic, minced	1
5 cups	chicken stock	1.25 L
3/4 tsp	dried thyme	4 mL
1/4 tsp	pepper	1 mL
1	can (19 oz/540 mL) lentils, drained	1
2 cups	quartered drained canned potatoes	500 mL
1	can (14 oz/398 mL) mixed vegetables, drained	1

● In large heavy saucepan, cook bacon over medium-high heat until crisp; remove and set aside.

● Add onion and garlic to pan; cook, stirring occasionally, for 3 minutes or until softened.

● Add chicken stock, thyme, pepper and bacon; bring to boil. Reduce heat, cover and simmer for 10 minutes. Add lentils, potatoes and vegetables; simmer, covered, for about 10 minutes or until steaming. Makes 5 servings.

*W*ith a cupboard stocked with canned lentils and vegetables, a main-course soup is ready in minutes.

Per serving: about
- 290 calories
- 10 g fat
- excellent source of iron
- 16 g protein
- 34 g carbohydrate
- high source of fiber

Italian Escarole Soup

8 cups	lightly packed coarsely chopped escarole	2 L
4 oz	prosciutto ham, in one piece	125 g
2 tbsp	olive oil	25 mL
2	onions, chopped	2
4	cloves garlic, minced	4
5 cups	chicken stock	1.25 L
1/2 tsp	pepper	2 mL
1/2 cup	stellini (star pasta) or other small soup noodle	125 mL
1 cup	fresh or frozen peas	250 mL
	Freshly grated Parmesan cheese (optional)	

● Wash escarole; drain. Place in large heavy saucepan with just the water clinging to leaves; cover and cook, stirring once, for 5 to 8 minutes or until wilted. Drain; squeeze out excess liquid. Chop finely and set aside.

● Trim any fat from prosciutto; chop finely. In same saucepan, heat oil over medium heat; cook onions, garlic and prosciutto, stirring often, for 5 to 10 minutes or until onions are softened.

● Stir in chicken stock, 1 cup (250 mL) water and pepper; bring to boil. Add pasta and escarole; reduce heat to medium-low and simmer for 3 minutes.

● Add peas; cook for 1 to 2 minutes or until peas and pasta are tender. Ladle into warmed bowls; sprinkle with Parmesan (if using). Makes 4 servings.

*E*scarole is lettuce with color and body. It is often added just at the last minute to brothy summer soups to brighten the bowl and take advantage of abundant greens.

Per serving: about
- 295 calories
- 11 g fat
- good source of iron
- 18 g protein
- 30 g carbohydrate
- high source of fiber

TIP: Escarole, with its frilly pale green leaves, is a sturdy green with a sharp flavor. If unavailable, substitute curly endive, which has finer and narrower leaves and a slightly more bitter flavor.

Vegetable Beef Minestrone ▶

This is a great feed-the-gang sort of soup based on ground beef with plenty of vegetables, tomatoes, chick-peas or beans of your choice plus pasta.

Per serving: about
- 450 calories
- 10 g fat
- excellent source of iron
- 27 g protein
- 66 g carbohydrate
- very high source of fiber

2	strips lean bacon, chopped	2
8 oz	lean ground beef	250 g
2	carrots, chopped	2
2	cloves garlic, minced	2
1	large onion, chopped	1
1	stalk celery, chopped	1
1	bay leaf	1
1 tsp	each dried basil and rosemary	5 mL
1/4 tsp	hot pepper flakes	1 mL
1	can (19 oz/540 mL) stewed tomatoes	1
1	can (10 oz/284 mL) beef stock	1
1	can (19 oz/540 mL) chick-peas, drained and rinsed	1
1 cup	broken spaghetti	250 mL
	Shaved Parmesan cheese (optional)	

● In large heavy saucepan, cook bacon over medium-high heat until crisp; drain off fat. Add beef; cook, breaking up with wooden spoon, for about 5 minutes or until no longer pink. Drain off fat.

● Add carrots, garlic, onion, celery, bay leaf, basil, rosemary and hot pepper flakes; cook, stirring occasionally, for about 5 minutes or until slightly softened.

● Stir in tomatoes, beef stock and 2-1/2 cups (625 mL) water; bring to boil. Reduce heat, cover and simmer for about 20 minutes or until vegetables are tender-crisp.

● Add chick-peas and spaghetti; cook, covered, for about 10 minutes or until spaghetti is tender. Discard bay leaf. Ladle into warmed bowls; sprinkle with Parmesan (if using). Makes 4 servings.

Oxtail Soup

Oxtail adds an unbeatable beef flavor to any soup, and the gelatin in the bones acts as a natural thickener. If refrigerated overnight, the fat in the soup rises and hardens, making it easy to lift off and discard.

Per serving: about
- 250 calories
- 10 g fat
- good source of iron
- 24 g protein
- 15 g carbohydrate

3	strips bacon, chopped	3
3 lb	oxtails	1.5 kg
3/4 tsp	each salt and pepper	4 mL
2	each onions, carrots and stalks celery, chopped	2
4	cloves garlic, minced	4
1 tsp	dried thyme	5 mL
8 cups	beef stock	2 L
1/4 cup	red wine vinegar	50 mL
3	each bay leaves and whole cloves	3
1/2 cup	rice	125 mL

● In large heavy saucepan, cook bacon over medium-high heat until crisp; transfer with slotted spoon to paper towel.

● Trim fat from oxtails. Sprinkle with 1/4 tsp (1 mL) each of the salt and pepper; add to pan and brown over medium-high heat on all sides, about 10 minutes. Transfer to plate.

● Drain off all but 1 tsp (5 mL) fat from pan; reduce heat to medium. Cook onions, carrots, celery, garlic and thyme, stirring occasionally, for about 8 minutes or until softened.

● Add beef stock, 1 cup (250 mL) water, vinegar and remaining salt and pepper, stirring to scrape up brown bits. Tie bay leaves and cloves in small square of cheesecloth; add to pan.

● Return oxtails and bacon to pan; bring to boil. Reduce heat, cover and simmer, turning oxtails occasionally, for 2 hours. Skim off fat.

● Add rice; bring to boil. Reduce heat and simmer, covered, for 15 minutes or until tender. Discard cheesecloth bag. Transfer oxtails to cutting board; cut off meat and return to pan. Discard bones. Makes 8 servings.

Slow-Cooker Tomato Vegetable Soup

The big benefit with this slow-cooker soup is assembling the ingredients in the morning so all you have to do when you get home is add the pasta.

Per serving: about
- 250 calories
- 8 g fat
- good source of iron
- 13 g protein
- 34 g carbohydrate
- high source of fiber

1	can (28 oz/796 mL) stewed tomatoes	1
2	each carrots and stalks celery, sliced	2
2	cloves garlic, minced	2
1	onion, chopped	1
1	can (19 oz/540 mL) chick-peas, drained and rinsed	1
1-1/2 cups	chopped cabbage	375 mL
6 oz	chunk of lean smoky bacon	175 g
1-1/2 tsp	dried basil	7 mL
1/4 tsp	each salt and pepper	1 mL
6 cups	chicken stock	1.5 L
1 cup	rotini pasta	250 mL
1/4 cup	chopped fresh parsley	50 mL

● In 18- to 24-cup (4.5 to 6 L) slow-cooker, mash tomatoes. Add carrots, celery, garlic, onion, chick-peas, cabbage, bacon, basil, salt and pepper. Stir in chicken stock. Cover and cook on low for 9 to 10 hours or until vegetables are tender.

● Add rotini; cook for 15 minutes or until tender. Remove bacon; chop and return to soup to reheat. Ladle into warmed bowls; sprinkle with parsley. Makes 6 servings.

Beefy Ratatouille Soup

Eggplant rounds out this soup's Provençale harvest flavors. Not fond of eggplant? Just double the zucchini, instead.

Per serving: about
- 245 calories
- 10 g fat
- excellent source of iron
- 20 g protein
- 21 g carbohydrate
- high source of fiber

1 tsp	vegetable oil	5 mL
12 oz	lean ground beef	375 g
1	onion, chopped	1
1	small eggplant, peeled and cubed	1
2	small zucchini, chopped	2
1	sweet red pepper, chopped	1
2	cloves garlic, minced	2
2 tsp	dried basil	10 mL
1/2 tsp	dried thyme	2 mL
1/4 tsp	each hot pepper flakes, salt and pepper	1 mL
2 cups	beef stock	500 mL
1	can (28 oz/796 mL) tomatoes, chopped	1
1	bay leaf	1

● In large heavy saucepan, heat oil over medium-high heat; cook beef, breaking up with back of spoon, for about 5 minutes or until no longer pink. Drain off fat.

● Add onion, eggplant, zucchini, red pepper, garlic, basil, thyme, hot pepper flakes, salt and pepper; cover and cook over medium heat, stirring occasionally, for about 5 minutes or just until vegetables are softened.

● Add beef stock, tomatoes with juices and bay leaf; bring to boil. Reduce heat to medium-low; cover and simmer for about 15 minutes or until vegetables are tender. Discard bay leaf. Makes 4 servings.

TIP: In summer, use 2-1/2 cups (625 mL) chopped fresh tomatoes instead of stewed, add a sprinkle more herbs and cook for about 10 minutes longer.

Quick Beef and Barley Soup

2 tsp	vegetable oil	10 mL
1	onion, chopped	1
2	carrots, sliced	2
2	stalks celery, sliced	2
2 cups	cubed peeled rutabaga	500 mL
1/4 cup	pot or pearl barley	50 mL
1/4 tsp	each dried thyme, dillweed and pepper	1 mL
1	can (10 oz/284 mL) beef stock	1
1-1/2 cups	cubed cooked beef	375 mL
1/4 cup	chopped fresh parsley	50 mL

● In large heavy saucepan, heat oil over medium heat; cook onion, carrots, celery and rutabaga, stirring occasionally, for about 3 minutes or until onion is softened. Stir in barley, thyme, dill and pepper until barley is coated.

● Stir in beef stock and 3 cups (750 mL) water; bring to boil. Cover and reduce heat to simmer; cook for about 45 minutes or until barley is tender.

● Add beef; cook for 5 minutes or until bubbly. Ladle into warmed bowls; sprinkle with parsley. Makes 4 servings.

Faster than the soup your granny simmered for hours, this updated version fits into today's lighter, quicker way of eating.

Per serving: about
- 240 calories
- 8 g fat
- good source of iron
- 20 g protein
- 23 g carbohydrate
- high source of fiber

TIP: Chopped peeled turnip, parsnip, sweet potato or squash can be added along with the carrots and rutabaga or used instead of them. Or, replace rutabaga with sliced mushrooms. If desired, add frozen peas or tiny broccoli florets when adding the beef.

Ginger Beef Consommé

2 tsp	sesame oil	10 mL
8 oz	stir-fry beef strips	250 g
1/2 cup	sliced water chestnuts, slivered	125 mL
4 tsp	minced gingerroot	20 mL
3	green onions, finely chopped	3
Pinch	hot pepper flakes	Pinch
1	can (10 oz/284 mL) beef stock	1
2 tbsp	sherry	25 mL
2 tbsp	chopped fresh coriander	25 mL

● In large heavy saucepan, heat half of the oil over medium-high heat; stir-fry beef, in two batches, for 1 to 2 minutes or just until browned but still pink inside. Transfer to plate.

● Wipe out pan. Heat remaining oil over medium heat; stir-fry water chestnuts, ginger, onions and hot pepper flakes for 2 minutes.

● Pour in beef stock, 2-1/2 cups (625 mL) water and sherry; bring to boil, skimming off foam. Reduce heat and simmer for 10 minutes.

● Drain beef; add to pan and simmer for 5 minutes. Ladle into warmed bowls; sprinkle with coriander. Makes 4 servings.

Stir-fried beef and beef broth are intensified with bold Asian flavors — dark sesame oil, pungent fresh gingerroot and fresh coriander.

Per serving: about
- 120 calories
- 4 g fat
- 14 g protein
- 6 g carbohydrate

TIP: If you can't find ready-cut stir-fry beef strips, slice inside round or sirloin tip very thinly across the grain. Chilling or partially freezing the meat makes slicing easier.

Satisfying Stews

Stews are the most forgiving of all dishes. You start with flavorful but (dare it be said) less than tender cuts of meat and let time and aromatic liquids work their magic to produce stellar dishes — juicy ones that beg for a bed of rice, pasta or couscous, a mound of mashed potatoes or polenta or that proverbial loaf of crusty bread.

Coconut Curried Chicken ▶

Fall in love with Asian flavors as you enjoy the tweak of chili paste and curry, mellowed by coconut milk and sharpened with lime. Make the effort to find basmati or Thai jasmine rice for the extra aroma and taste they add to Eastern dishes.

Per serving: about
- 390 calories
- 24 g fat
- excellent source of iron
- 27 g protein
- 22 g carbohydrate
- high source of fiber

3	boneless skinless chicken breasts (1 lb/ 500 g)	3
1 tbsp	vegetable oil	15 mL
1 tbsp	Indian medium curry paste or curry powder	15 mL
2	cloves garlic, minced	2
2 tsp	grated lime rind	10 mL
1-1/2 tsp	each ground coriander and ground cumin	7 mL
1/4 tsp	chili paste or hot pepper sauce	1 mL
1/2 tsp	each granulated sugar and salt	2 mL
1/4 tsp	pepper	1 mL
3 cups	quartered mushrooms (about 8 oz/250 g)	750 mL
2	carrots, diagonally sliced	2
1	onion, sliced	1
3 tbsp	lime juice	50 mL
1-1/2 cups	coconut milk	375 mL
2	tomatoes, chopped	2
1 cup	frozen peas	250 mL
1/4 cup	chopped fresh coriander	50 mL

● Cut chicken into bite-size chunks. In large heavy saucepan, heat 2 tsp (10 mL) of the oil over medium-high heat; cook chicken, stirring often, for 5 minutes or just until no longer pink inside. Transfer to plate.

● Add remaining oil to pan; reduce heat to medium. Add curry paste, garlic, lime rind, ground coriander, cumin, chili paste, sugar, salt and pepper; cook, stirring, for 30 seconds.

● Add mushrooms, carrots, onion and lime juice; cook, stirring occasionally, for 10 minutes or until mushrooms start to turn golden and liquid is evaporated.

● Pour in coconut milk and bring to boil; boil for 5 minutes. Reduce heat to medium. Stir in tomatoes and reserved chicken; cook for 3 minutes. Stir in peas, heat through and add fresh coriander. Makes 4 servings.

Chicken and Squash Stew with Prunes

For this powerhouse of flavor and delicious sauce, choose a delicata squash or half a butternut and serve over couscous or rice.

Per serving: about
- 375 calories
- 10 g fat
- excellent source of iron
- 32 g protein
- 43 g carbohydrate
- very high source of fiber

8	small chicken thighs (about 1-1/3 lb/675 g)	8
1	squash (1 lb/500 g)	1
1 tbsp	vegetable oil	15 mL
1	onion, chopped	1
3	cloves garlic, minced	3
4 tsp	all-purpose flour	20 mL
1 tsp	ground coriander or ground cumin	5 mL
3/4 tsp	ground ginger	4 mL
1/2 tsp	cinnamon	2 mL
3/4 cup	chicken stock	175 mL
1	can (19 oz/540 mL) tomatoes	1
1 cup	pitted prunes	250 mL
2 tbsp	chopped fresh parsley	25 mL

● Skin chicken thighs; trim any visible fat. Peel and seed squash; cut into 1-inch (2.5 cm) cubes to make 3 cups (750 mL).

● In large heavy saucepan, heat oil over medium-high heat; brown chicken all over, in batches, about 6 minutes. Transfer to plate.

● Reduce heat to medium. Add onion and garlic; cook for about 3 minutes or until softened. Add flour, coriander, ginger and cinnamon; cook, stirring, for 1 minute. Stir in squash and chicken stock. Add tomatoes, breaking up with spoon. Bring to boil.

● Return chicken and any juices to pan; reduce heat, cover and simmer for 20 minutes. Add prunes and parsley; cook, uncovered, for about 10 minutes or until thickened and squash is tender. Makes 4 servings.

Caribbean Chicken Stew

Take your tastebuds on tour with this make-ahead mild curry to spoon over noodles or rice.

Per serving: about
- 345 calories
- 10 g fat
- good source of iron
- 25 g protein
- 38 g carbohydrate
- high source of fiber

10	chicken thighs (2 lb/1 kg)	10
3 tbsp	all-purpose flour	50 mL
1/2 tsp	each salt and pepper	2 mL
2 tbsp	vegetable oil	25 mL
1	large onion, chopped	1
2	cloves garlic, minced	2
2	jalapeño peppers, seeded and finely chopped (or 1/4 tsp/1 mL hot pepper flakes)	2
1-1/2 tsp	curry powder	7 mL
1 tsp	dried thyme	5 mL
1/2 tsp	dried marjoram	2 mL
1-1/2 cups	chicken stock	375 mL
3	sweet potatoes (about 1-3/4 lb/875 g)	3
2	zucchini	2
1/4 cup	chopped fresh coriander or parsley	50 mL

● Skin chicken thighs; trim any visible fat. In plastic bag, combine flour, salt and pepper. In batches, add chicken; shake to coat. In large heavy saucepan, heat half of the oil over medium-high heat; brown chicken all over, about 6 minutes. Transfer to plate.

● Add remaining oil to pan; reduce heat to medium. Add onion, garlic, jalapeños, curry powder, thyme and marjoram; cook, stirring occasionally, for 5 minutes or until onion is softened. Add chicken stock; bring to boil. Return chicken and any juices to pan; cover and simmer for 20 minutes.

● Meanwhile, peel and quarter sweet potatoes; cut into 2-inch (5 cm) chunks. Quarter zucchini lengthwise; cut into 2-inch (5 cm) lengths. Add potatoes to pan; simmer, covered, for 15 minutes. Add zucchini; cook for 5 to 7 minutes or until vegetables are tender and juices run clear when chicken is pierced. Stir in coriander. Makes 5 servings.

Chicken Stew in a Hurry ▲

3	boneless skinless chicken breasts (1 lb/500 g)	3
3/4 tsp	salt	4 mL
1/2 tsp	each dried thyme and pepper	2 mL
1 tbsp	vegetable oil	15 mL
4 cups	frozen mixed chopped vegetables	1 L
1	can (385 mL) evaporated skim milk	1
1 tbsp	cornstarch	15 mL
1-1/2 tsp	Dijon mustard	7 mL
1	pkg (212 g) refrigerated buttermilk biscuit dough	1

● Cut chicken into 1/2-inch (1 cm) cubes; sprinkle with salt, thyme and pepper. In large heavy saucepan, heat oil over medium-high heat; brown chicken all over, in batches if necessary. Reduce heat to medium. Add vegetables; cook, stirring often, for 10 minutes or until liquid is evaporated.

● Whisk together evaporated milk, cornstarch and mustard; pour into pan and bring to boil over medium-high heat, stirring. Reduce heat to medium; cook, stirring often, for about 10 minutes or until sauce is thickened and chicken is no longer pink inside.

● Meanwhile, bake biscuits according to package directions. Cut in half crosswise; place 2 bottom halves on each plate. Spoon stew over biscuits; top with remaining halves. Makes 4 servings.

S*core three times on the convenience scale with frozen mixed vegetables, refrigerator biscuit dough and the friend of everyone in a rush — boneless, skinless chicken breasts.*

Per serving: about
- 490 calories
- 7 g fat
- good source of iron
- excellent source of calcium
- 42 g protein
- 64 g carbohydrate
- very high source of fiber

Chicken with Pasta and Peppers ▼

Easy as one, two, three: brown chicken, cook onion with seasonings, add tomatoes and sauce — then simmer until done.

Per each of 6 servings: about
- 505 calories
- 16 g fat
- good source of iron
- 32 g protein
- 57 g carbohydrate
- high source of fiber

1 tbsp	olive oil	15 mL
2 lb	chicken parts	1 kg
2	onions, chopped	2
2	cloves garlic, minced	2
1 tsp	dried basil	5 mL
1/2 tsp	each dried oregano and thyme	2 mL
1	can (19 oz/540 mL) tomatoes	1
1	can (14 oz/398 mL) tomato sauce	1
2 cups	coarsely chopped sweet peppers	500 mL
	Salt and pepper	
12 oz	rotini or spaghetti	375 g
	Fresh basil leaves	

● In large heavy saucepan, heat oil over medium-high heat; brown chicken all over, in batches, about 10 minutes. Transfer to plate.

● Reduce heat to medium. Add onions, garlic, dried basil, oregano and thyme; cook, stirring, for 3 minutes. Add tomatoes, breaking up with fork; add tomato sauce.

● Return chicken and any accumulated juices to pan; bring to boil. Reduce heat and simmer, turning chicken and stirring occasionally, for 30 minutes. Add peppers; cook for 5 to 10 minutes or until juices run clear when chicken is pierced. Season with salt and pepper to taste.

● Meanwhile, in large pot of boiling salted water, cook pasta for about 8 minutes or until tender but firm; drain and arrange on serving plate. Top with chicken mixture; garnish with fresh basil. Makes 4 to 6 servings.

Chicken Paprikash

3	slices bacon	3
6	whole chicken legs, skinned (about 3 lb/1.5 kg)	6
1	large onion, chopped	1
2	cloves garlic, minced	2
3	carrots, chopped	3
1	each sweet red and green pepper, chopped	1
3 tbsp	sweet Hungarian paprika	50 mL
1 tbsp	all-purpose flour	15 mL
1 tsp	salt	5 mL
1/2 tsp	each dried thyme and pepper	2 mL
1 cup	chicken stock	250 mL
1/4 cup	tomato paste	50 mL
Dash	hot pepper sauce (optional)	Dash
3/4 cup	sour cream	175 mL
2 tbsp	chopped fresh parsley	25 mL

● In large heavy saucepan, cook bacon over medium-high heat until well browned and crisp. Using tongs, transfer to paper towel and let cool. Crumble into bits; set aside.

● Drain off all but 1 tbsp (15 mL) fat from pan. Add chicken, in batches if necessary, and brown all over until golden. Transfer to plate.

● Add onion and garlic to pan; cook, stirring occasionally, for 3 minutes or until softened. Add carrots, red and green peppers, paprika, flour, salt, thyme and pepper; cook, stirring, for 2 minutes.

● Add chicken stock, tomato paste, and hot pepper sauce (if using). Return chicken and any accumulated juices to pan; bring to boil, stirring to scrape up any brown bits. Reduce heat, cover and simmer for 40 minutes or until juices run clear when chicken is pierced. Remove chicken from pan and keep warm.

● Stir sour cream into pan; simmer, stirring, for about 5 minutes or until sauce is thickened. Serve over chicken. Garnish with parsley and reserved bacon. Makes 6 servings.

Here's another delicious way to brown and simmer chicken that's wonderfully economical and, best of all, tasty and satisfying. Take the cue from the paprika flavor and serve over egg noodles.

Per serving: about
- 310 calories
- 14 g fat
- good source of iron
- 31 g protein
- 16 g carbohydrate

WHEN MAKING STEWS OR SOUPS AHEAD

A stash of stew or soup in the fridge or freezer is like money in the bank for a hungry household. And making these dishes in volume makes sense when leftovers provide such good lunches, satisfying suppers and emergency meals. Here are a few tips for getting the best out of your make-ahead soups and stews.

● A large pot of soup or stew takes too long to cool off safely at room temperature. Transfer contents to shallow container(s) and chill as quickly as possible in the refrigerator. Lift off any congealed fat. Divide into containers that suit your household. Refrigerate, covered, for up to 2 days or freeze in airtight freezer containers. Most of these juicy dishes will have a freezer life of about one month.

● Always thaw frozen dishes in the refrigerator.

● Soups and stews containing potatoes and fennel do not freeze well. Freeze without these ingredients, then add them when reheating dish.

● Tender greens such as spinach or Swiss chard, added at the last minute, should be reserved for the reheating time.

● Pasta and rice continue to absorb liquid when frozen in a soup or stew. They expand and soften. If time permits, add these ingredients at reheating time.

● Make your stew look like new the second time around by dressing it up under a corn bread crust (p. 66), a blanket of dumplings (p. 70), or over your favorite biscuits or popovers.

Chicken Cacciatore

This quick chicken stew with tomatoes and mushrooms is delicious with crusty bread, but equally nice with mashed potatoes, polenta or a short pasta such as rotini. What's especially pleasing about this Italian classic is its expandability, making it ideal for inexpensive entertaining.

Per each of 6 servings: about
- 250 calories
- 9 g fat
- good source of iron
- 22 g protein
- 21 g carbohydrate
- high source of fiber

1/4 cup	all-purpose flour	50 mL
1/4 tsp	each salt and pepper	1 mL
8	chicken thighs, skinned (about 2 lb/1 kg)	8
2 tbsp	vegetable oil	25 mL
1	large onion, chopped	1
2	cloves garlic, minced	2
2	carrots, chopped	2
1	sweet green pepper, chopped	1
3 cups	sliced mushrooms (about 8 oz/250 g)	750 mL
1 tsp	dried marjoram	5 mL
1 tsp	grated lemon rind	5 mL
1/2 tsp	dried rosemary	2 mL
1	can (19 oz/540 mL) tomatoes, chopped	1
1	can (14 oz/398 mL) tomato sauce	1
1/4 cup	red wine (or 2 tbsp/25 mL red wine vinegar)	50 mL
2	bay leaves	2
2 tbsp	chopped fresh parsley	25 mL

● In shallow dish or plastic bag, combine flour, salt and pepper. Add chicken, in batches, and shake to coat well. Reserve any remaining flour mixture.

● In large heavy saucepan, heat oil over medium-high heat; brown chicken all over, in batches, 7 to 10 minutes. Remove and set aside.

● Reduce heat to medium. Add onion, garlic, carrots, green pepper and mushrooms; cook, stirring often, for about 10 minutes or until liquid is evaporated and mushrooms start to turn golden.

● Add marjoram, lemon rind, rosemary and any reserved flour mixture; cook, stirring, for 1 minute. Add tomatoes, tomato sauce, wine and bay leaves; bring to boil. Reduce heat and simmer for about 35 minutes or until sauce is thickened and juices run clear when chicken is pierced. Discard bay leaves. Serve garnished with parsley. Makes 4 to 6 servings.

Chicken à la King

Aren't you glad old-fashioned comfort food is back? Make this with either chicken or turkey, and serve it in patty shells or on toast or split tea biscuits.

Per serving: about
- 350 calories
- 25 g fat
- 24 g protein
- 8 g carbohydrate

3 tbsp	butter	50 mL
3/4 cup	sliced mushrooms	175 mL
1/4 cup	each chopped onion and celery	50 mL
1/4 cup	chopped sweet green pepper	50 mL
2 tbsp	all-purpose flour	25 mL
1 cup	18% cream	250 mL
1/2 cup	chicken stock	125 mL
1 tbsp	dry sherry (optional)	15 mL
	Salt and pepper	
2 cups	cubed cooked chicken (see p. 38)	500 mL
2 tbsp	chopped pimiento	25 mL

● In large heavy saucepan, melt 1 tbsp (15 mL) of the butter over medium heat; cook mushrooms, onion, celery and green pepper, stirring occasionally, just until tender. With slotted spoon, remove vegetable mixture and set aside.

● Melt remaining butter in pan; stir in flour until bubbling. Stir in cream and chicken stock; cook, stirring constantly, until boiling and thickened. Cook for 2 minutes longer. Stir in sherry (if using). Season with salt and pepper to taste.

● Stir in reserved vegetable mixture, chicken and pimiento; cook, stirring occasionally, until heated through. Makes 4 servings.

Microwave Turkey Gumbo Stew ▼

2 tbsp	all-purpose flour	25 mL
1 tbsp	vegetable oil	15 mL
1 cup	chopped onions	250 mL
1	stalk celery, diced	1
1	sweet green pepper, diced	1
1	can (19 oz/540 mL) tomatoes	1
1 cup	turkey or chicken stock	250 mL
1/4 cup	long grain rice	50 mL
2	cloves garlic, minced	2
1 tsp	dried oregano	5 mL
1/2 tsp	pepper	2 mL
1 cup	partially thawed okra or peas	250 mL
1-1/2 cups	cubed cooked turkey	375 mL
	Salt	
	Hot pepper sauce	

● In 12-cup (3 L) microwaveable casserole, mix flour with oil; microwave, uncovered, at High for 8 to 10 minutes or until golden, stirring 3 times.

● Stir in onions, celery and green pepper; microwave at High for 4 to 6 minutes or until softened, stirring once.

● Add tomatoes, turkey stock, rice, garlic, oregano and pepper; cover and microwave at High for 15 to 20 minutes or until rice is tender, stirring twice and breaking up tomatoes.

● Cut okra into bite-size pieces; add to pot. Stir in turkey; cover and microwave at High for 2 minutes or until heated through. Season with salt and hot pepper sauce to taste. Makes 4 servings.

*T*urkey goes Cajun in a spicy and satisfying soup that will have everyone asking for seconds.

Per serving: about
- 250 calories
- 7 g fat
- good source of iron
- 21 g protein
- 27 g carbohydrate

TIP: Cajun gumbos are thickened with a dark roux, an oil-and-flour mixture that is cooked until golden. Microwaving the roux eliminates the constant stirring of stove-top cooking.

Osso Buco ◀

6	thick (1-1/2-inch/4 cm) pieces veal hind shank (3-1/2 lb/1.75 kg)	6
2 tbsp	all-purpose flour	25 mL
1/2 tsp	each salt and pepper	2 mL
2 tbsp	olive oil (approx)	25 mL
1 cup	each chopped onion and carrot	250 mL
2/3 cup	chopped celery	150 mL
2	cloves garlic, minced	2
3/4 tsp	dried sage	4 mL
1/2 tsp	dried thyme	2 mL
1/4 tsp	dried rosemary	1 mL
3/4 cup	dry white wine	175 mL
1-1/2 cups	canned tomatoes, coarsely chopped	375 mL
1/2 cup	beef stock	125 mL
2	bay leaves	2
	GREMOLATA TOPPING	
1	lemon	1
1	clove garlic, minced	1
1/4 cup	chopped fresh parsley	50 mL

● Cut six 24-inch (60 cm) lengths of kitchen string; wrap each twice around each shank and tie firmly. On plate, combine flour and half each of the salt and pepper; press shanks into mixture to coat both sides well. Reserve any remaining flour mixture.

● In Dutch oven large enough to hold shanks in single layer, heat oil over medium-heat; brown shanks all over, in batches if necessary, adding up to 1 tbsp (15 mL) more

oil if necessary. Transfer to plate. Drain fat from pan.

● Add onion, carrot, celery, garlic, sage, thyme and rosemary to pan; cook over medium heat, stirring often, for 10 minutes. Sprinkle with reserved flour; cook, stirring, for 1 minute. Add wine, scraping up brown bits. Bring to boil; boil for 2 minutes or until reduced by half.

● Stir in tomatoes, beef stock, bay leaves and remaining salt and pepper. Nestle shanks in mixture; bring to boil. Cover and bake in 350°F (180°C) oven, basting every 30 minutes, for 1-1/2 hours. Turn meat and bake, uncovered and basting twice, for 30 minutes or until tender and sauce is thickened.

● Transfer shanks to platter; cut off string and keep warm. Place pan over medium-high heat; boil gently, stirring, for about 5 minutes or until desired thickness. Discard bay leaves. Pour sauce over shanks.

● GREMOLATA TOPPING: Meanwhile, finely grate lemon rind. In small bowl, stir together lemon rind, garlic and parsley; sprinkle over shanks. Makes 6 servings.

VARIATION

● CHICKEN OSSO BUCO: Replace veal with 12 skinned chicken thighs, and beef stock with chicken stock. Omit rosemary. Cook, covered, for 1 hour and uncovered for 15 minutes only. Omit boiling sauce for 5 minutes.

*C*osy up to brisk weather with saucy veal shanks braised with tomatoes, herbs, wine and vegetables.

Per serving: about
- 555 calories
- 24 g fat
- excellent source of iron
- 64 g protein
- 16 g carbohydrate

STEW BASICS

1 Dusting meat in flour is called dredging and it helps to brown the meat quickly and intensely. Flour also provides thickening, turning flavorful cooking liquid into gravy.

2 Searing and browning meat for a stew develops deep rich flavor through caramelization, which permeates the dish during its long simmer. Brown meat in batches. Adding too much meat to the pan at one time will cause meat to steam, not brown nicely.

3 When adding liquid, scrape up the flavorful brown bits from the bottom of the pan with a wooden spoon. These bits dissolve and enrich the dish.

Curried Beef Stew with Chick-Peas

*Curry paste, like curry
powder, comes mild, medium
and hot. Choose the degree of
heat you enjoy.*

Per serving: about
- 275 calories
- 10 g fat
- good source
  of iron
- 23 g protein
- 23 g carbohydrate
- high source
  of fiber

1 lb	stew beef	500 g
4 tsp	vegetable oil	20 mL
2	onions, chopped	2
2	large cloves garlic, minced	2
1 tbsp	minced gingerroot	15 mL
1 tbsp	curry paste (hot, medium or mild)	15 mL
1/2 tsp	each ground coriander and ground cumin	2 mL
1/4 tsp	cinnamon	1 mL
1	can (19 oz/540 mL) tomatoes	1
1 tbsp	lemon juice	15 mL
2 tsp	dried mint	10 mL
1	hot green chili, sliced	1
1	can (19 oz/540 mL) chick-peas, drained and rinsed	1
2 tbsp	finely chopped fresh coriander	25 mL

● If necessary, cut beef into 1-inch (2.5 cm) cubes, trimming off any fat. In large heavy saucepan, heat 1 tbsp (15 mL) of the oil over medium-high heat; brown beef all over, in batches. Transfer to plate.

● In same pan, heat remaining oil over low heat; cook onions, garlic, ginger, curry paste, ground coriander, cumin and cinnamon, stirring, for 6 minutes or until onions are tender.

● Add tomatoes, breaking up with spoon. Return beef and any accumulated juices to pan. Add lemon juice, mint and green chili; bring to boil. Reduce heat, cover and simmer gently for 30 minutes.

● Stir in chick-peas; cover and simmer, stirring occasionally, for about 30 minutes or until beef is tender. If desired, uncover and simmer until sauce is thickened. Sprinkle with coriander. Makes 6 servings.

TIP: Curry paste, which comes in jars, has a mellow, rounded spicy flavor, preferable to many of the curry powders on the market. Once opened, the jar should be stored in the refrigerator where it will keep for months.

Tagine of Beef with Prunes ▶

*Moroccan stews take their
name from the conical-shape
pottery dish they're cooked
in. Enjoy with couscous or
warmed flatbreads such as
pita. A tart salad of sliced
oranges, black olives and red
onions complements the
sweetness of a typical tangine.*

Per serving: about
- 450 calories
- 15 g fat
- excellent
  source of iron
- 30 g protein
- 51 g carbohydrate
- very high source
  of fiber

1-1/2 lb	stew beef	750 g
1/4 cup	all-purpose flour	50 mL
1/2 tsp	salt	2 mL
2 tbsp	olive or vegetable oil	25 mL
4	onions, quartered	4
4	cloves garlic, sliced	4
3	large carrots, chopped	3
1	stalk celery, sliced	1
2 tsp	ground cumin	10 mL
1 tsp	each ground coriander and paprika	5 mL
1/4 tsp	each cinnamon and cayenne pepper	1 mL
2-1/2 cups	beef stock	625 mL

1/4 cup	tomato paste	50 mL
1 tbsp	red wine vinegar	15 mL
1	orange	1
2 cups	pitted prunes	500 mL
1/4 cup	each chopped fresh parsley and green onion	50 mL

● If necessary, cut beef into bite-size cubes, trimming off any fat. In shallow dish, combine flour with salt; add beef, turning to coat all over. In large heavy saucepan, heat half of the oil over medium-high heat; brown beef all over, in batches, about 10 minutes. Transfer to plate.

● Add remaining oil to pan; reduce heat to medium. Add onions, garlic, carrots, celery, cumin, coriander, paprika, cinnamon and cayenne pepper; cook, stirring often, for about 8 minutes or until vegetables are softened.

● Return beef and any accumulated juices to pan. Add beef stock, tomato paste and vinegar. Cut off 2 long strips of orange rind; add to pan. Squeeze juice from orange to make 1/3 cup (75 mL); add to pan. Bring to boil; reduce heat, cover and simmer for 1-1/2 hours, stirring occasionally.

● Add prunes; simmer for 30 minutes or until beef is tender, uncovering if necessary to thicken sauce. Serve sprinkled with parsley and green onion. Makes 6 servings.

Beef Bourguignonne with Noodles ◄

3 lb	stew beef	1.5 kg
2 tbsp	vegetable oil	25 mL
1	Spanish onion, minced	1
7 cups	halved mushrooms	1.75 L
3	cloves garlic, minced	3
1/2 tsp	each dried thyme, salt and pepper	2 mL
1/4 cup	all-purpose flour	50 mL
1-1/2 cups	each red wine and hot beef stock	375 mL
1	bay leaf	1
1-1/2 lb	noodles or other pasta	750 g
1/4 cup	chopped fresh parsley	50 mL

● If necessary, cut beef into bite-size cubes, trimming off any fat. In large heavy saucepan, heat 1 tbsp (15 mL) of the oil over medium-high heat; brown beef all over, in batches and adding remaining oil as necessary. Transfer to plate.

● Add onion, mushrooms, garlic, thyme, salt and pepper to pan; cook over medium heat, stirring occasionally, for about 8 minutes or until onion is softened and liquid is evaporated.

● Return beef and any accumulated juices to pan. Sprinkle with flour; cook, stirring, for 1 minute. Add wine, beef stock and bay leaf; bring to boil. Reduce heat, cover and simmer for 2-1/2 hours. Uncover and cook for 30 minutes or until thickened and meat is tender. Discard bay leaf.

● Meanwhile, in large pot of boiling salted water, cook noodles for 8 to 10 minutes or until tender but firm; drain well. Divide among plates. Spoon bourguignonne over top; sprinkle with parsley. Makes 6 to 8 servings.

A classic for good reason, and a favorite of Olympian Gaétan Boucher. Serve vegetables alongside.

Per each of 8 servings: about
- 695 calories
- 20 g fat
- excellent source of iron
- 50 g protein
- 75 g carbohydrate
- high source of fiber

Peter Gzowski's Caribou Stew

1-1/2 lb	stewing caribou	750 g
1/2 cup	all-purpose flour	125 mL
1/4 tsp	pepper	1 mL
2 tbsp	each butter and olive oil	25 mL
3	onions, cut in 8 wedges each	3
3	leeks (white parts only), chopped	3
5	cloves garlic, minced	5
1 tsp	dried oregano	5 mL
1/2 tsp	dried basil	2 mL
1-1/2 cups	beef stock	375 mL
1/2 cup	dry sherry	125 mL
4	carrots, chopped	4
1	can (19 oz/540 mL) tomatoes	1
4	parsnips, chopped	4
12	small new potatoes (1-1/2 lb/750 g), scrubbed	12
	Salt	
1/4 cup	chopped fresh parsley	50 mL

● Trim any fat from caribou; cut meat into 1-1/2-inch (4 cm) cubes. In paper bag, shake flour with pepper; add meat, one-third at a time, and shake to coat well.

● In large heavy saucepan, heat butter with oil over medium-high heat; brown beef, in batches. Transfer to plate.

● Reduce heat to medium. Add onions, leeks, garlic, oregano and basil; cook, stirring occasionally, for 5 minutes. Pour in beef stock, 1 cup (250 mL) water and sherry; bring to boil, stirring to scrape up any brown bits.

● Return meat and any accumulated juices to pan. Add carrots; cover and simmer for 1 hour. Add tomatoes, breaking up with fork. Add parsnips; cook, partially covered, for 20 minutes. Add potatoes; cook for about 30 minutes or until caribou and potatoes are tender. Season with salt to taste. Serve garnished with parsley. Makes 6 servings.

Northern readers of Peter Gzowski's column in Canadian Living responded to his acclaimed beef stew recipe with this game version. Try it if you have access to caribou; otherwise, substitute beef and you'll still enjoy the stew.

Per serving: about
- 510 calories
- 13 g fat
- excellent source of iron
- 30 g protein
- 65 g carbohydrate
- very high source of fiber

Oh-So-Easy Stew

Because beef stew is so simple to make, anyone can succeed and even get raves.

Per serving: about
- 545 calories
- 15 g fat
- excellent source of iron
- good source of calcium
- 35 g protein
- 70 g carbohydrate
- very high source of fiber

1 lb	stew beef	500 g
1/4 cup	all-purpose flour	50 mL
1/2 tsp	salt	2 mL
1/4 tsp	pepper	1 mL
1 tbsp	vegetable oil (approx)	15 mL
2	onions, chopped	2
2	cloves garlic, minced	2
1 tsp	dried thyme	5 mL
1/2 tsp	dried oregano	2 mL
1	bay leaf	1
4	large carrots	4
2	stalks celery	2
Half	small rutabaga, peeled	Half
2 cups	beef stock	500 mL
1	can (19 oz/540 mL) tomatoes	1
4	potatoes, peeled and quartered	4
1 cup	frozen peas or beans	250 mL
1 tbsp	red wine vinegar	15 mL
1/4 cup	chopped fresh parsley	50 mL

● If necessary, cut beef into bite-size cubes, trimming off fat. In heavy plastic bag, shake together flour, salt and pepper. Add beef, in batches, and shake to coat, reserving any remaining flour.

● In Dutch oven, heat oil over medium-high heat; brown beef all over, in batches and adding up to 1 tbsp (15 mL) more oil if necessary. Transfer to plate.

● Reduce heat to medium-low. Add onions, garlic, thyme, oregano, bay leaf and remaining flour to pan; cook, stirring to scrape up brown bits, for 5 minutes or until onions are softened. Return beef and any accumulated juices to pan.

● Meanwhile, cut carrots, celery and rutabaga into 2-inch (5 cm) chunks; add to pan. Add beef stock and tomatoes; bring to boil. Reduce heat, cover and simmer over medium-low heat for 1-1/2 hours. Add potatoes; cook, covered, for 1 hour or until tender. Add peas and vinegar; cook for 2 minutes. Discard bay leaf. Stir in parsley. Makes 4 servings.

Bavarian Beef

Every country has its favorite flavor combinations with beef. In southern Germany, there's caraway, a touch of spice and a bay leaf. Serve a tangy red cabbage salad alongside.

Per serving: about
- 375 calories
- 15 g fat
- excellent source of iron
- 35 g protein
- 24 g carbohydrate

2 lb	stew beef	1 kg
1 tbsp	vegetable oil	15 mL
2 cups	chopped onions	500 mL
2 tsp	caraway seeds	10 mL
1/4 tsp	pepper	1 mL
1	bay leaf	1
2 cups	beef stock	500 mL
1/3 cup	red wine vinegar	75 mL
3 tbsp	packed brown sugar	50 mL
1 tbsp	grated lemon rind	15 mL
1/4 cup	molasses	50 mL
2 tbsp	all-purpose flour	25 mL
1 tsp	each ground ginger and cinnamon	5 mL
1/4 tsp	ground cloves	1 mL

● If necessary, cut beef into bite-size cubes, trimming off any fat. In large heavy saucepan, heat oil over medium-high heat; brown beef all over, in batches. Transfer to plate.

● Add onions, caraway seeds, pepper and bay leaf to pan; cook, stirring, for 1 minute. Pour in beef stock; bring to boil, stirring to scrape up brown bits.

● Return beef and any accumulated juices to pan; reduce heat, cover and simmer for 2 hours or until beef is tender. Stir in vinegar, sugar and lemon rind; cook, uncovered and stirring often, for 30 minutes.

● In small bowl, stir together molasses, flour, ginger, cinnamon and cloves to make paste; stir in 2 tbsp (25 mL) of the stew juices. Increase heat to high. Gradually whisk molasses mixture into stew, stirring until thickened, 3 to 5 minutes. Discard bay leaf. Makes 6 servings.

Apple and Sweet Potato Beef Curry

1 tbsp	vegetable oil	15 mL
2	cloves garlic, minced	2
1	onion, finely chopped	1
1 cup	cubed peeled sweet potato	250 mL
1 lb	lean ground beef	500 g
1 tbsp	each curry powder and ground cumin	15 mL
1/2 tsp	each cinnamon and salt	2 mL
1/4 tsp	each pepper and hot pepper flakes	1 mL
1	can (28 oz/796 mL) tomatoes, chopped	1
1 tbsp	liquid honey	15 mL
2	apples, peeled and diced	2
	Fresh coriander sprigs	

● In large heavy saucepan, heat oil over medium heat; cook garlic, onion, sweet potato and 2 tbsp (25 mL) water, stirring often, for 5 minutes.

● Add beef, breaking up with wooden spoon; cook for about 5 minutes or until no longer pink. Add curry powder, cumin, cinnamon, salt, pepper and hot pepper flakes; cook, stirring, for 2 minutes.

● Add tomatoes with juices and honey; simmer, stirring occasionally, for 15 minutes. Add apples; cook for about 10 minutes or until tender and curry is thickened. Serve garnished with coriander. Makes 6 servings.

Lean ground beef is the starting point for a colorful curry that's quick enough for Monday-to-Friday suppers.

Per serving: about
- 285 calories
- 15 g fat
- excellent source of iron
- 16 g protein
- 24 g carbohydrate

Autumn Beef Stew

2 lb	stew beef	1 kg
1 tbsp	olive oil	15 mL
2	onions, coarsely chopped	2
2	cloves garlic, minced	2
1	large sweet green pepper, coarsely chopped	1
1-1/2 cups	beef stock	375 mL
1/4 cup	Madeira wine	50 mL
1	large ripe tomato, peeled and coarsely chopped	1
1 tsp	salt	5 mL
1/2 tsp	pepper	2 mL
3	sweet potatoes, peeled and cut in 1-inch (2.5 cm) cubes	3
2 cups	frozen corn kernels	500 mL
1/2 cup	dried apricots, halved	125 mL
1/3 cup	dried pitted prunes	75 mL

● If necessary, cut beef into 1-inch (2.5 cm) cubes, trimming off any fat. In large heavy saucepan, heat oil over medium-high heat; brown beef all over, in batches. Transfer to plate.

● Reduce heat to medium. Add onions, garlic and green pepper; cook, stirring often, for about 5 minutes or until softened.

● Return beef and any accumulated juices to pan. Add beef stock and Madeira; bring to boil, stirring to scrape up brown bits from bottom of pan. Add tomato, salt and pepper; return to boil. Reduce heat, cover and simmer for 45 minutes.

● Stir in sweet potatoes; simmer, uncovered and stirring occasionally, for 30 minutes. Stir in corn, apricots and prunes; simmer for 30 minutes or until meat is tender. Makes 6 servings.

The wonderfully hospitable food writer and author, Rose Murray, includes everything from apricots and prunes to beef and potatoes in this great party dish that has its origins in Argentina.

Per serving: about
- 475 calories
- 16 g fat
- excellent source of iron
- 38 g protein
- 46 g carbohydrate
- very high source of fiber

FOR A SPECTACULAR PRESENTATION
Complete the cooking of the stew in a pumpkin large enough to hold 10 cups (2.5 L) after hollowing out. Cut off pumpkin top for lid; remove seeds and membranes. Place on foil-lined rimmed baking sheet. After stew has simmered for 1 hour, spoon into pumpkin and cover with lid; bake in 325°F (160°C) oven for 1 hour or until beef is tender and pumpkin is tender enough to be scooped (but not mushy). Serve from pumpkin.

Slow-Cooker Barbecue Beef Stew ▲

There's a tasty hit of barbecue-sauce flavor in this family-pleasing stew. While the stew is thickening, cook a pot of noodles.

Per serving: about
- 480 calories
- 17 g fat
- excellent source of iron
- 54 g protein
- 27 g carbohydrate

2 lb	stew beef	1 kg
2	onions, sliced	2
2	cloves garlic, minced	2
1/2 cup	chili sauce	125 mL
2 tbsp	packed brown sugar	25 mL
2 tbsp	Worcestershire sauce	25 mL
1 tbsp	paprika	15 mL
1 tsp	dried marjoram	5 mL
1/2 tsp	each dry mustard and salt	2 mL
1/4 tsp	pepper	1 mL
3 tbsp	all-purpose flour	50 mL

● If necessary, cut beef into bite-size cubes, trimming off any fat. Place in 18- to 24-cup (4.5 to 6 L) slow cooker. Sprinkle with onions and garlic.

● Stir together 1 cup (250 mL) water, chili sauce, sugar, Worcestershire sauce, paprika, marjoram, mustard, salt and pepper; pour over beef. Cover and cook on low for 8 to 10 hours or until meat is tender.

● Stir flour into 1/4 cup (50 mL) cold water; stir into meat mixture. Increase heat to high; cover and cook for 10 to 15 minutes or until thickened. Makes 4 servings.

Rosemary Beef Ragout

1 lb	stew beef	500 g
4 tsp	olive oil	20 mL
2	onions, chopped	2
3	cloves garlic, minced	3
1-1/2 tsp	crumbled dried rosemary	7 mL
2 tbsp	balsamic or red wine vinegar	25 mL
2 tbsp	all-purpose flour	25 mL
3-1/2 cups	beef stock	875 mL
2 tbsp	tomato paste	25 mL
1/2 tsp	each salt and pepper	2 mL
5	carrots, peeled and thickly sliced	5
1	large fennel bulb	1
4	potatoes, peeled and cut in 1-inch (2.5 cm) cubes	4
1/4 cup	chopped fresh parsley	50 mL

● If necessary, cut beef into 1-inch (2.5 cm) cubes, trimming off any fat. In large heavy saucepan, heat half of the oil over high heat; brown beef all over, in batches. Transfer to plate.

● Add remaining oil to pan; reduce heat to medium. Add onions, garlic and rosemary; cook, stirring, for 5 minutes or until softened. Add vinegar; cook for 2 minutes or until liquid is almost evaporated. Sprinkle with flour. Add beef stock, tomato paste, salt and pepper; bring to boil. Cook, stirring, for about 4 minutes or until slightly thickened.

● Return meat and any accumulated juices to pan; reduce heat, cover and simmer for 45 minutes. Add carrots; simmer, covered, for 30 minutes. Meanwhile, trim top from fennel; cut in half lengthwise and remove core. Cut in half crosswise; cut into thin strips lengthwise.

● Add fennel and potatoes to pan; simmer, covered, for 25 to 30 minutes or until beef and vegetables are tender. Stir in parsley. Makes 4 servings.

Rosemary gives a distinct yet not overpowering flavor that nicely balances the sweet-sour balsamic vinegar.

Per serving: about
- 475 calories
- 16 g fat
- excellent source of iron
- 33 g protein
- 53 g carbohydrate
- very high source of fiber

TIP: If you can't find fennel, substitute 1-1/2 cups (375 mL) sliced celery.

People's Choice Chili

7	strips lean bacon	7
1 lb	lean ground beef	500 g
1	onion, chopped	1
1	clove garlic, minced	1
2 tbsp	packed brown sugar	25 mL
2 tbsp	fancy molasses	25 mL
1	can (19 oz/540 mL) tomatoes	1
1	can (14 oz/398 mL) kidney beans	1
1	can (14 oz/398 mL) pork and beans	1
1/3 cup	vinegar	75 mL
1 tsp	dry mustard	5 mL
1 tsp	Worcestershire sauce	5 mL
1/2 tsp	salt	2 mL
1/4 tsp	each pepper and hot pepper sauce	1 mL

● In Dutch oven, cook bacon over medium-high heat until crisp. Drain on paper towels; crumble and set aside.

● Drain fat from pan. Add beef and onion; cook, breaking up meat with wooden spoon, for 10 minutes or until no longer pink. Drain off fat.

● Return bacon to pan. Add garlic, sugar, molasses, tomatoes, kidney beans, pork and beans, vinegar, mustard, Worcestershire sauce, salt, pepper and hot pepper sauce; stir well. Cover and bake in 300°F (150°C) oven for 2 hours. Uncover and bake for 1 hour longer or until thickened. Makes 4 servings.

No, there's no chili powder in this chili. But there are beans, and this chili has won the People's Choice Award for the last six years at Stratford, Ontario's, Heartburn Day. The winning Oliver Rubber Company team contributes gallons of this mild chili to the charity fundraising day.

Per serving: about
- 575 calories
- 21 g fat
- excellent source of iron
- 39 g protein
- 61 g carbohydrate
- very high source of fiber

Beefy Chick-Pea and Sausage Chili

*Chick-peas and sausage
pair with beef to update a
long-standing family favorite.
Serve over baked potatoes —
or blanket chili with corn
bread (see recipe, below) and
bake together.*

Per serving: about
- 315 calories
- 25 g protein
- 15 g fat
- 20 g carbohydrate
- excellent
  source of iron

8 oz	fresh Italian or chorizo sausage, thinly sliced	250 g
1-1/2 lb	lean ground beef	750 g
2	stalks celery, chopped	2
2	cloves garlic, chopped	2
1	large onion, chopped	1
1	sweet green pepper, chopped	1
1	carrot, chopped	1
1 tbsp	chili powder	15 mL
1 tsp	each ground cumin and dried oregano	5 mL
1/2 tsp	salt	2 mL
1/4 tsp	cayenne pepper	1 mL
1	can (28 oz/796 mL) tomatoes	1
1	can (19 oz/540 mL) chick-peas, drained and rinsed	1

● In large heavy saucepan, brown sausage over medium-high heat, about 8 minutes; transfer to plate. Drain fat from pan. Add beef; cook, breaking up with wooden spoon, for about 7 minutes or until no longer pink. Drain off any fat.

● Return sausage to pan; reduce heat to medium. Add celery, garlic, onion, green pepper, carrot, chili powder, cumin, oregano, salt and cayenne pepper; cook, stirring often, for about 8 minutes or until vegetables are softened.

● Add tomatoes, crushing with fork; bring to boil. Reduce heat, cover and simmer, stirring occasionally, for 1 hour.

● Add chick-peas; simmer, uncovered and stirring occasionally, for about 30 minutes or until chili is thickened. Makes 8 servings.

Corn Bread Chili ▶

*Use the delicious corn bread
topping with any of your
favorite chilis.*

Per each of 6 servings: about
- 390 calories
- 24 g protein
- 18 g fat
- 33 g carbohydrate
- good source
  of iron and
  calcium

**FREEZING
CHILI**

Chili can be frozen in
convenient amounts in
airtight containers for up
to 1 month.

4 cups	Beefy Chick-Pea and Sausage Chili (recipe, above)	1 L
	CORN BREAD TOPPING	
1/2 cup	all-purpose flour	125 mL
1/4 cup	cornmeal	50 mL
1 tsp	baking powder	5 mL
1/4 tsp	baking soda	1 mL
1/4 tsp	each salt and pepper	1 mL
2	green onions, sliced	2
1 cup	corn kernels	250 mL
1/2 cup	buttermilk	125 mL
1	egg	1
1 tbsp	chopped canned green chilies	15 mL
1 tbsp	vegetable oil	15 mL
3/4 cup	shredded Cheddar cheese	375 mL

● Pour chili into 8-inch (2 L) square baking dish; set aside.

● CORN BREAD TOPPING: In bowl, combine flour, cornmeal, baking powder, baking soda, salt, pepper and green onions. In separate bowl, whisk together corn, buttermilk, egg, green chilies and oil; pour over flour mixture. Stir just until dry ingredients are moistened.

● Spread cornmeal mixture evenly over chili. Sprinkle with cheese. Bake in 400°F (200°C) oven for 35 to 45 minutes or until bubbly and corn bread is golden on top and no longer doughy underneath. Makes 4 to 6 servings.

Spicy Sausage and Black Bean Chili ▲

W*elcome to the world of zesty chili, pepped up with lots of chili powder and chipotle peppers (dried smoked jalapeño) canned in a tangy tomato sauce (adobo). Black beans add to the new twists.*

Per serving: about
- 370 calories
- 16 g fat
- excellent source of iron
- 23 g protein
- 36 g carbohydrate
- very high source of fiber

1 lb	hot Italian sausage	500 g
2 tbsp	chili powder	25 mL
2 tsp	each ground cumin and dried oregano	10 mL
1 tsp	cinnamon	5 mL
1 tsp	fennel seeds, crushed	5 mL
2	bay leaves	2
2	onions, chopped	2
4	cloves garlic, minced	4
2	sweet red peppers, diced	2
1	chipotle pepper, diced	1
1 tsp	adobo sauce	5 mL
1	can (28 oz/796 mL) diced tomatoes	1
1	can (19 oz/540 mL) black beans, drained and rinsed	1

● Remove sausage from casings. In large heavy saucepan, brown sausage over medium-high heat, mashing to separate meat. Drain off all but 2 tsp (10 mL) fat.

● Reduce heat to medium. Add chili powder, cumin, oregano, cinnamon, fennel seeds and bay leaves; cook, stirring, for 1 minute. Add onions, garlic, red peppers, chipotle pepper and adobo sauce; cook, stirring, for 8 minutes or until vegetables are softened.

● Stir in tomatoes and 3 cups (750 mL) water; bring to boil. Reduce heat, cover and simmer, stirring occasionally, for 20 minutes. Stir in beans; simmer, uncovered and stirring often, for about 30 minutes or until sauce is thickened. Discard bay leaves. Makes 5 servings.

TIP: You can replace the chipotle pepper and adobo sauce with 2 tbsp (25 mL) diced fresh or pickled jalapeño pepper, or hot pepper sauce to taste.

Chunky Beef and Pork Chili with Beer

2 lb	boneless cross-rib steak, trimmed	1 kg
1 lb	lean boneless pork	500 g
2 tbsp	vegetable oil	25 mL
3 tbsp	chili powder	50 mL
2 tbsp	ground cumin	25 mL
2 tsp	dried oregano	10 mL
2 tsp	paprika	10 mL
1/2 tsp	ground coriander	2 mL
1/4 tsp	cayenne pepper	1 mL
2	onions, chopped	2
4	cloves garlic, slivered	4
2-1/2 cups	beef stock	625 mL
1	bottle (12 oz/341 mL) beer	1
1/4 cup	tomato paste	50 mL
2 tsp	granulated sugar	10 mL
2 tsp	unsweetened cocoa powder	10 mL
	GARNISH	
1 cup	diced sweet green pepper	250 mL
1/4 cup	sliced green onions	50 mL
1/4 cup	chopped fresh coriander	50 mL

● Cut beef and pork into 3/4-inch (2 cm) cubes, trimming off any fat. In large heavy saucepan, heat half of the oil over medium-high heat; brown meat all over, in batches and adding remaining oil as necessary. Transfer to plate.

● Drain off any fat in pan; reduce heat to medium. Add chili powder, cumin, oregano, paprika, coriander and cayenne pepper; cook, stirring, for 1 minute. Add onions and garlic; cook, stirring occasionally, for about 5 minutes or until softened.

● Return meat and any accumulated juices to pan. Blend in beef stock, beer, tomato paste, sugar and cocoa powder; bring to boil. Reduce heat, cover and simmer, stirring often, for 1-1/2 hours or until meat is tender, uncovering for last 30 minutes if necessary to thicken.

● GARNISH: Toss together green pepper, green onions and coriander; sprinkle over each serving. Makes 6 servings.

This all-meat chili is dark and rich, and especially delectable spooned over a baked sweet or white potato.

Per serving: about
- 395 calories
- 18 g fat
- excellent source of iron
- 44 g protein
- 15 g carbohydrate

Bean Pot on the Run

1	ham bone or ham hock	1
2 cups	tomato juice	500 mL
1	onion, chopped	1
1	sweet green pepper, chopped	1
4	whole cloves	4
2	cans (each 14 oz/398 mL) baked beans	2
1	can (19 oz/540 mL) kidney beans, drained and rinsed	1
1 tbsp	each Worcestershire sauce and wine vinegar	15 mL
1 tsp	dry mustard	5 mL

● In large heavy saucepan, combine ham bone, tomato juice, onion, green pepper and cloves; bring to boil. Reduce heat and simmer for 30 minutes.

● Remove bone from pan; cut away any meat. Discard bone and cloves. Return meat to pan along with baked beans, kidney beans, Worcestershire sauce, vinegar and mustard; bring to boil. Reduce heat and simmer for about 20 minutes or until sauce is thickened. Makes 4 servings.

A bone-in ham is a treasure. You can roast the whole ham or cut the meat into steaks for a barbecue, serve slivers with pasta or a stir-fry, make sandwiches, and feel thrifty simmering the bone with beans. If you don't have a ham bone, use 8 oz (250 g) smoked sausage, sliced.

Per serving: about
- 455 calories
- 8 g fat
- excellent source of iron
- 31 g protein
- 72 g carbohydrate
- very high source of fiber

Quebec Pot-au-Feu

*The Montreal Gazette's
Julian Armstrong dipped into
regional Quebec cooking for
these braised short ribs
flavored with eastern
Canada's favorite herb —
summer savory.*

Per serving: about
- 215 calories
- 15 g protein
- 10 g fat
- 15 g carbohydrate

2	strips bacon	2
2 lb	beef short ribs	1 kg
2	onions, sliced	2
5 cups	beef stock	1.25 L
2	tomatoes, peeled, seeded and chopped	2
1 tsp	dried savory	5 mL
1	bay leaf	1
6	whole cloves	6
1 cup	cubed peeled turnip or rutabaga	250 mL
3	carrots, sliced	3
2	potatoes, peeled and cubed	2
1 tsp	salt	5 mL
1/2 tsp	pepper	2 mL
1 tbsp	all-purpose flour	15 mL
1 tbsp	butter, softened	15 mL
	Chopped fresh parsley	

● In large heavy saucepan, cook bacon over medium-high heat until crisp. Drain on paper towels; crumble and set aside. Drain off fat from pan, reserving 2 tbsp (25 mL).

● Cut ribs into 2-inch (5 cm) pieces, trimming off any fat. Heat 1 tbsp (15 mL) of the reserved fat in pan; brown ribs all over, in batches and without crowding, adding remaining reserved fat if necessary. Transfer to plate.

● Drain off all but 1 tbsp (15 mL) fat from pan. Add onions; cook, stirring often, for about 5 minutes or until golden. Add 1 cup (250 mL) of the beef stock, stirring to scrape up brown bits from bottom of pan.

● Return short ribs and bacon to pan; add remaining beef stock, tomatoes, savory and bay leaf. Tie cloves in small square of cheesecloth; add to pan. Bring to boil; reduce heat to low, cover and simmer for 1-1/2 hours.

● Add turnip, carrots and potatoes; cook for 15 to 20 minutes or until tender. Discard bay leaf and cloves. Season with salt and pepper.

● Mix flour with butter; stir into beef mixture and cook, stirring, for 3 minutes or until thickened. Sprinkle with parsley. Makes 8 servings.

TIP: To reduce fat, trim ribs of visible fat, then finish by skimming any fat from surface of stew; or chill it, then remove solidified fat.

HERBED BUTTERMILK DUMPLINGS

Cake-and-pastry flour makes light, delicate dumplings for topping any hearty stew.

2 cups	sifted cake-and-pastry flour	500 mL
1 tsp	baking powder	5 mL
1/2 tsp	baking soda	2 mL
1/4 tsp	salt	1 mL
2 tbsp	butter or shortening	25 mL
1/4 cup	chopped fresh parsley	50 mL
1 tsp	chopped fresh thyme (or 1/4 tsp/1 mL dried), optional	5 mL
3/4 cup	buttermilk	175 mL

● In large bowl, stir or whisk together flour, baking powder, baking soda and salt. With pastry blender or two knives, cut in butter until mixture is crumbly. Stir in parsley, and thyme (if using). Drizzle with buttermilk, stirring with fork to make soft dough.

● Spoon onto hot stew, placing dough on pieces of meat or vegetables rather than into liquid. Cover and simmer, without lifting lid, for about 15 minutes or until dumplings are puffed and no longer doughy on bottom. Makes 6 large dumplings.

Per dumpling: about • 180 calories • 4 g protein • 5 g fat
• 30 g carbohydrate • good source of iron

Pork Carbonnade

2-1/2 lb	boneless pork shoulder butt	1.25 kg
4	onions	4
1/4 cup	all-purpose flour	50 mL
1 tsp	dry mustard	5 mL
1/2 tsp	each salt and pepper	2 mL
6	strips lean bacon	6
2	cloves garlic, minced	2
1 tbsp	packed brown sugar	15 mL
1 tsp	dried thyme	5 mL
1	bottle (12 oz/341 mL) beer	1
1/2 cup	chicken stock	125 mL
1 tbsp	Worcestershire sauce	15 mL
1 tbsp	cider vinegar	15 mL

● Trim any fat from pork; cut meat into 1-inch (2.5 cm) cubes. Cut each onion into 8 wedges; set aside. In shallow dish or plastic bag, combine flour, mustard, salt and pepper. Add pork, in batches, and shake to coat well. Reserve any remaining flour mixture.

● In Dutch oven, cook bacon over medium-high heat for about 3 minutes or until fat is released. Using tongs, transfer bacon to paper towel and let cool; chop and set aside. Drain off all but 1 tbsp (15 mL) fat from pan. Brown pork, in batches; transfer to plate.

● Reduce heat to medium. Add onions, garlic, brown sugar, thyme and any reserved flour mixture to pan; cook, stirring often, for 10 minutes or until onions are softened.

● Return bacon and pork and any accumulated juices to pan. Blend in beer, chicken stock, Worcestershire sauce and vinegar; bring to boil, stirring to scrape up any brown bits. Cover and bake in 350°F (180°C) oven for 45 minutes. Uncover, stir and bake for 30 minutes or until pork is tender and sauce is thickened slightly. Makes 6 servings.

The appetizing bitterness of beer balances the sweetness of slow-cooked onions in a hearty stew that's sure to take the chill off a fall or winter day.

Per serving: about
• 385 calories
• 19 g fat
• good source of iron
• 35 g protein
• 16 g carbohydrate

Basque Pork Stew

2 lb	lean pork shoulder	1 kg
3 tbsp	olive oil	50 mL
	Salt and pepper	
2	onions, thickly sliced	2
1 cup	chicken stock	250 mL
2 tbsp	tomato paste	25 mL
2	sweet red peppers, cut in strips	2
4 oz	prosciutto or ham, coarsely chopped	125 g
10	cloves garlic, thinly sliced	10
1 tsp	each paprika and dried thyme	5 mL
1/4 tsp	hot pepper flakes	1 mL
1	orange	1

● Trim any fat from pork; cut meat into 1-1/2-inch (4 cm) cubes. In large heavy saucepan, heat 1 tbsp (15 mL) of the oil over medium-high heat; brown pork all over, in batches and adding more oil as necessary. Sprinkle with salt and pepper to taste. Transfer to plate.

● Reduce heat to medium. Add onions to pan; cook, stirring occasionally, for 5 minutes. Add chicken stock and tomato paste; bring to boil, scraping up any brown bits. Return pork and any accumulated juices to pan; stir in red peppers, prosciutto, garlic, paprika, thyme and hot pepper flakes.

● Grate rind from orange; add to stew. Peel orange; chop coarsely and stir into stew. Reduce heat to low; cover and simmer, stirring occasionally, for 1 to 1-1/2 hours or until pork is tender. Makes 4 servings.

Citrusy chunks of succulent pork and bright peppers — the Basque influence — bring a little sunshine to the dinner table. Serve over rice, with steamed broccoli.

Per serving: about
• 520 calories
• 24 g fat
• excellent source of iron
• 56 g protein
• 19 g carbohydrate
• high source of fiber

Pork Vindaloo

A southern Indian-style pork stew includes the tang of vinegar. This is an ideal way to use succulent and very affordable pork shoulder.

Per serving: about
- 405 calories
- 50 g protein
- 18 g fat
- 9 g carbohydrate
- excellent source of iron

3 lb	lean boneless pork shoulder butt	1.5 kg
2 tbsp	all-purpose flour	25 mL
2 tsp	ground cumin	10 mL
1-1/2 tsp	each ground coriander and turmeric	7 mL
3/4 tsp	ground cardamom	4 mL
1/4 tsp	each ground cinnamon, salt and pepper	1 mL
Pinch	ground cloves	Pinch
2 tbsp	vegetable oil	25 mL
2	onions, chopped	2
6	cloves garlic, sliced	6
1/4 cup	white vinegar	50 mL
1 tbsp	minced gingerroot	15 mL
1 tbsp	grainy mustard	15 mL
1/4 tsp	hot pepper flakes	1 mL
2 cups	chicken stock	500 mL
2	bay leaves	2

● Trim any fat from pork; cut meat into 1-1/2-inch (4 cm) cubes. Place in bowl. In separate bowl, mix together flour, cumin, coriander, turmeric, cardamom, cinnamon, salt, pepper and cloves; sprinkle half over pork, tossing to coat well.

● In large heavy saucepan, heat half of the oil over medium-high heat; brown pork, in batches and adding more oil as necessary. Transfer to plate.

● Add remaining oil to pan; reduce heat to medium. Add remaining spice mixture, onions, garlic, 2 tbsp (25 mL) of the vinegar, ginger, mustard and hot pepper flakes; cook, stirring, for about 6 minutes or until onions are softened.

● Pour in chicken stock and remaining vinegar; bring to boil, stirring to scrape up any brown bits. Return pork and any accumulated juices to pan; add bay leaves. Reduce heat, cover and simmer, stirring occasionally, for 30 minutes. Uncover and simmer for about 15 minutes or until pork is tender and sauce is thickened. Discard bay leaves. Makes 6 servings.

Thai Curry Pork Stew ▶

The distinctive flavors of Thai cooking — fish sauce is certainly one of them, and prepared Thai curry paste is another — make this a memorable stew to serve with rice and a side dish of sliced mangoes.

Per serving: about
- 265 calories
- 28 g protein
- 9 g fat
- 19 g carbohydrate
- good source of iron

1 lb	boneless pork shoulder butt	500 g
1 tbsp	vegetable oil	15 mL
1 tbsp	Thai red curry paste	15 mL
2	onions, cut in wedges	2
2	cloves garlic, minced	2
2 tbsp	chopped gingerroot	25 mL
2 tsp	grated lime rind	10 mL
2 tbsp	lime juice	25 mL
2 tbsp	fish sauce	25 mL
1 tbsp	granulated sugar	15 mL
1/4 tsp	salt	1 mL
8 oz	green beans	250 g

1-1/2 cups	cauliflower florets	375 mL
1	sweet red pepper	1
2 tbsp	each chopped fresh mint and coriander	25 mL

● Trim any fat from pork; cut meat into 2-inch (5 cm) cubes. In large heavy saucepan, heat 2 tsp (10 mL) of the oil over medium-high heat; brown meat, in batches. Transfer to plate.

● Reduce heat to medium; add remaining oil to pan. Add curry paste; cook for 1 minute, mashing paste into oil. Add onions, garlic and ginger; cook, stirring, for 1 minute.

● Add lime rind, lime juice, fish sauce, sugar, salt and 1 cup (250 mL) water; bring to boil.

● Return meat and any accumulated juices to pan. Reduce heat, cover and simmer, stirring occasionally, for about 40 minutes or until meat is very tender.

● Meanwhile, trim green beans; cut in half crosswise. Add to pan along with cauliflower; cook, covered, over medium heat for 10 minutes.

● Meanwhile, core, seed and cut red pepper in half crosswise; cut lengthwise into strips. Add to pan;

cook, uncovered and stirring often, for about 5 minutes or until vegetables are tender. Stir in mint and coriander. Makes 4 servings.

Pork Ragout with Sweet Potatoes ▶

After a day of skiing or tobogganing, invite the gang back for nourishing bowlfuls of this hearty meat-and-potatoes stew.

Per serving: about
- 525 calories
- 15 g fat
- excellent source of iron
- 40 g protein
- 53 g carbohydrate
- high source of fibre

3 lb	boneless pork shoulder butt	1.5 kg
1/3 cup	packed brown sugar	75 mL
1/3 cup	all-purpose flour	75 mL
1/4 cup	Dijon mustard	50 mL
3 tbsp	vegetable oil	50 mL
1	onion, chopped	1
2	cloves garlic, minced	2
1-1/3 cups	chicken stock	325 mL
1 cup	dry sherry	250 mL
6	sweet potatoes (about 3 lb/1.5 kg)	6
1/2 tsp	each salt and pepper	2 mL
1/4 cup	chopped fresh parsley	50 mL

● Trim any fat from pork; cut meat into 1-inch (2.5 cm) cubes. In shallow dish, combine sugar with flour. Coat pork lightly in mustard; roll in sugar mixture to coat all over.

● In large nonstick skillet, heat oil over medium heat; brown pork, in batches. With slotted spoon, transfer to large Dutch oven. Add onion and garlic to skillet; cook, stirring often, for 3 minutes. Transfer with slotted spoon to Dutch oven.

● Drain off any fat in skillet. Pour in chicken stock and sherry; bring to boil and boil for 1 minute, stirring to scrape up browned bits. Add to Dutch oven.

● Peel sweet potatoes; cut into 1-inch (2.5 cm) cubes. In large saucepan of boiling water, cook potatoes for 3 minutes or until barely tender. Drain and add to Dutch oven.

● Cover and bake in 350°F (180°C) oven for about 45 minutes or until meat is tender. Add salt and pepper. Sprinkle with parsley. Makes 8 servings.

Ragoût de Boulettes

A Quebec warmer-upper shows a great technique for dark rich sauces — toasting the flour before blending it into the stew to thicken.

Per each of 8 servings: about
- 330 calories
- 20 g fat
- 25 g protein
- 12 g carbohydrate

2	slices white bread	2
1/2 cup	milk	125 mL
2 tbsp	butter	25 mL
3/4 cup	minced onion	175 mL
2 lb	lean ground pork	1 kg
3 tbsp	minced fresh parsley	50 mL
2 tsp	salt	10 mL
1 tsp	dry mustard	5 mL
1/2 tsp	each cinnamon and pepper	2 mL
1/4 tsp	each ground cloves, ginger and nutmeg	1 mL
4 cups	beef or chicken stock	1 L
1/2 cup	all-purpose flour	125 mL
	Finely chopped fresh parsley (optional)	

● Crumb or cube bread very finely; soak in milk for 5 minutes.

● In large skillet, melt 1 tbsp (15 mL) of the butter over medium heat; cook onion, stirring, for about 3 minutes. Transfer to large bowl; add pork, bread mixture, parsley, salt, mustard, cinnamon, pepper, cloves, ginger and nutmeg. Mix thoroughly; form into 2-inch (5 cm) balls.

● In skillet, melt remaining butter over medium heat; brown meatballs, in batches. Transfer to large heavy saucepan; set aside.

● Drain off any fat in skillet. Pour in 1 cup (250 mL) of the stock and bring to boil, stirring to scrape up browned bits. Pour over meatballs along with remaining stock. Simmer, partially covered, for 1-1/4 hours.

● In clean skillet, cook flour over medium heat, stirring frequently, until golden. Transfer to jar with tight-fitting lid; add 3/4 cup (175 mL) cold water and shake until smooth. Gradually pour into stew, stirring constantly; cook until thickened. Simmer for 10 minutes. Sprinkle generously with parsley (if using). Makes 6 to 8 servings.

Greek Lamb and Bean Stew ◄

2 cups	dried large lima beans	500 mL
1 lb	lean boneless lamb	500 g
2 tbsp	olive oil	25 mL
1	Spanish onion (1 lb/500 g), chopped	1
4	cloves garlic, minced	4
1 tbsp	dried oregano	15 mL
1/2 tsp	hot pepper flakes	2 mL
1	can (19 oz/540 mL) tomatoes, chopped	1
1 tsp	salt	5 mL
1/2 tsp	pepper	2 mL
1	each large sweet red and green pepper, cubed	1
1/2 cup	kalamata olives, rinsed	125 mL
1/4 cup	chopped fresh parsley	50 mL

● Sort and rinse beans. In large saucepan, bring beans and 8 cups (2 L) cold water to boil; cover and cook for 15 minutes. Drain and return to pot.

● Add 8 cups (2 L) water; bring to boil. Reduce heat and simmer, partially covered, for 45 minutes or until tender. Drain.

● Meanwhile, trim any fat from lamb; cut meat into 1-inch (2.5 cm) cubes. In Dutch oven, heat half of the oil over high heat; brown lamb all over, in batches if necessary. Transfer to plate.

● Reduce heat to medium; add remaining oil to pan. Add onion, garlic, oregano and hot pepper flakes; cook, stirring, for 5 minutes or until softened. Return meat and any accumulated juices to pan. Add tomatoes, salt and pepper; bring to boil. Reduce heat, cover and simmer for 45 minutes.

● Add beans, red and green peppers, olives and about 1/2 cup (125 mL) water to make sauce-like consistency. Bake, covered, in 350°F (180°C) oven for about 40 minutes or until lamb is tender. Stir in parsley. Makes 4 servings.

Montrealer Johanna Burkhard created this stew with signature Greek ingredients — lamb, olives and oregano. The delectable surprise is the big, buttery lima beans.

Per serving: about
- 610 calories
- 19 g fat
- excellent source of iron
- 45 g protein
- 69 g carbohydrate
- very high source of fiber

TIP: Instead of soaking and pre-cooking dried lima beans, you can substitute 4 cups (1 L) thawed lima beans; add to stew as specified.

A Fine Lamb and Squash Stew

1 lb	boneless lamb shoulder	500 g
1/2 tsp	pepper	2 mL
2 tsp	vegetable oil	10 mL
1	onion, chopped	1
1	clove garlic, minced	1
1/2 tsp	paprika	2 mL
1-1/2 cups	beef stock	375 mL
1-1/2 tsp	dried mint	7 mL
1 tsp	grated lemon rind	5 mL
2 cups	cubed peeled squash	500 mL
8 oz	green beans	250 g
1 tbsp	red wine vinegar	15 mL

● Trim any fat from lamb; cut meat into bite-size cubes. Sprinkle with pepper. In large heavy saucepan, heat oil over medium-high heat; brown lamb all over, in batches if necessary. Transfer to plate. Drain off any fat in pan.

● Reduce heat to medium. Add onion, garlic and paprika to pan; cook, stirring occasionally, for 4 minutes or until softened.

● Add beef stock, mint and lemon rind; bring to boil, stirring to scrape up browned bits. Return lamb and any accumulated juices to pan; reduce heat, cover and simmer for 1 hour. Stir in squash; cover and simmer for about 15 minutes or until lamb is tender.

● Meanwhile, trim and cut beans into 1-inch (2.5 cm) pieces; add to stew and simmer for 12 to 15 minutes or until tender-crisp. Stir in vinegar. Makes 4 servings.

Boneless lamb shoulder, well trimmed before browning, is always the best choice for stewing. Because leg is so lean, it tends to be tough and stringy in a stew.

Per serving: about
- 200 calories
- 8 g fat
- good source of iron
- 20 g protein
- 15 g carbohydrate

Estouffade d'Agneau à la Provençale ▶

From *Le Passe-Partout*
restaurant and premier
bakery in Montreal comes this
glorious and finely made stew
sealed and baked with a ring
of bread dough.

Per serving: about
- 560 calories
- 38 g protein
- 25 g fat
- 42 g carbohydrate
- excellent
  source of iron

3 tbsp	olive oil	50 mL
2	onions, sliced	2
2-1/2 lb	boneless lamb shoulder	1.25 kg
1	each onion, carrot and stalk celery, chopped	1
1 tsp	dried thyme	5 mL
1/4 tsp	each salt and pepper	1 mL
1 cup	white wine	250 mL
1/2 cup	beef stock	125 mL
2 cups	diced plum tomatoes	500 mL
2	large cloves garlic, minced	2
1/3 cup	black olives (not canned)	75 mL
2 tbsp	brandy	25 mL
12 oz	pizza or bread dough	375 g

● In Dutch oven, heat 1 tbsp (15 mL) of the oil over medium-low heat; cook sliced onions, stirring often, for 10 minutes or until softened and beginning to color. Transfer to plate. Wipe out pan.

● Trim any fat from lamb; cut meat into bite-size cubes. Heat 2 tsp (10 mL) of the oil in pan over high heat; brown lamb, in batches and adding more oil as necessary. Transfer to separate plate.

● Reduce heat to medium. Add chopped onion, carrot, celery, thyme, salt and pepper; cook, stirring often and adding more oil if needed, until golden brown.

● Return lamb and any accumulated juices to pan. Add wine and beef stock; bring to boil. Cover and bake in 350°F (180°C) oven for 1 to 1-1/2 hours or until lamb is barely tender. Add sliced onions, tomatoes, garlic, olives and brandy; stir to combine.

● Uncover pan. Roll and stretch dough into rope long enough to circle rim of pan; press onto rim, making sure most of the dough is on outside. Place lid over dough; press gently but firmly to seal. Bake in 350°F (180°C) oven for about 40 minutes or until bread is crusty and golden. Serve bread in pieces with stew. Makes 6 servings.

TIP: If using a red enamelled cast-iron Dutch oven, line rim of pan with foil to prevent bread from touching the enamel.

STOCKS FOR STEWS AND SOUPS

In our recipes, we use the term *stock* instead of broth or bouillon because it is the generic word for all strained liquid that results from cooking vegetables, seasonings and poultry, meat or fish in water.

● Homemade stock is the best, and we've included recipes for the most versatile and easiest stocks to make: chicken, vegetable (see index) and fish. The major advantage to homemade stocks is the taste.

● For all these stocks plus beef stock, which is not as practical to make at home, there are powders, concentrates and cubes. While some of these instant stocks do capture the taste of their namesake, they are often very salty. Wherever possible, look for unsalted versions or use sparingly and omit or reduce salt or other salty ingredients in the recipe.

● Canned chicken and beef stocks usually have a meatier flavor but are salty. And while

these are handy — just open and pour — you have to work around a given amount. Freeze leftovers, if needed, for your next batch of soup.

● Fresh concentrated stocks, stored in the refrigerator, are worth investing in for the convenience of making just what you need.

Fish Stock

● To make your own, bring the following to a gentle boil and simmer for 30 minutes: 1 small onion, chopped, half a small leek, chopped,

1-1/2 lb (750 g) fish bones and heads, 2 stalks of parsley, 1 small bay leaf, pinch each dried dillweed and thyme, 3 peppercorns and 5 cups (1.25 L) water. Strain to make about 4 cups (1 L). Freeze in convenient airtight containers.

● Because chicken stock is mild, it can often replace fish stock. An equal mix of white wine and water is another alternative, as is clam juice mixed with an equal amount of water.

Lamb Shanks with Caramelized Onions

Stew recipes do look long, but almost all of the work for this entertaining stew is up front, so while it simmers, you can prepare side dishes or simply relax.

Per serving: about
- 530 calories
- 44 g protein
- 17 g fat
- 52 g carbohydrate
- excellent source of iron
- very high source of fiber

1 tbsp	vegetable oil	15 mL
6	lamb shanks	6
2	onions, chopped	2
3	cloves garlic, chopped	3
1-1/2 tsp	cinnamon	7 mL
1 tsp	paprika	5 mL
1/2 tsp	each salt, pepper and turmeric	2 mL
Pinch	hot pepper flakes	Pinch
4 cups	beef stock	1 L
1	can (19 oz/540 mL) tomatoes, coarsely chopped	1
3	large carrots, thickly sliced	3
4	zucchini, thickly sliced	4
1	can (19 oz/540 mL) chick-peas, drained and rinsed	1
	CARAMELIZED ONIONS	
2 tbsp	butter	25 mL
4	onions, sliced	4
1 tbsp	granulated sugar	15 mL
3/4 tsp	cinnamon	4 mL
1/2 tsp	ground ginger	2 mL
1/4 tsp	each salt, pepper and turmeric	1 mL
1/2 cup	raisins	125 mL
1/4 cup	slivered almonds, toasted	50 mL

● In large heavy saucepan, heat oil over medium-high heat; brown lamb shanks all over, in batches. Transfer to plate. Drain off any fat in pan.

● Reduce heat to medium. Add onions, garlic, cinnamon, paprika, salt, pepper, turmeric and hot pepper flakes to pan; cook, stirring often, for 5 minutes or until softened.

● Return shanks and any accumulated juices to pan. Add beef stock and tomatoes; bring to boil. Reduce heat, cover and simmer for about 1-1/2 hours or until lamb is just tender.

● Increase heat to medium. Add carrots, zucchini and chick-peas; simmer, covered, for about 20 minutes or until lamb and vegetables are tender.

● Strain, reserving liquid; set meat and vegetables aside. Return reserved liquid to pan; boil for about 15 minutes or until reduced to half. Return meat and vegetables to pan; heat through.

● CARAMELIZED ONIONS: Meanwhile, in large heavy skillet, melt butter over medium heat. Add onions, sugar, cinnamon, ginger, salt, pepper and turmeric; cover and cook, stirring occasionally, for 10 minutes. Add raisins; cook for 10 minutes. Uncover and cook, stirring occasionally, for about 5 minutes or until onions are golden and no liquid remains.

● Ladle stew into warmed bowls. Top with caramelized onions; sprinkle with almonds. Makes 6 servings.

THE RIGHT POT FOR STEWS

Browning is the most important flavor maker for stews. And for this, you need a shallow pot with a heavy bottom that ensures even heat distribution. A good Dutch oven is ideal because it can be used both over high heat on top of the stove for browning and in the oven for oven stewing or braising. Choose enameled cast iron or stainless steel with an aluminum sandwich base.

Cioppino

1/4 cup	olive oil	50 mL
2	onions, chopped	2
4	cloves garlic, minced	4
1	can (28 oz/796 mL) tomatoes, crushed	1
1	can (14 oz/398 mL) tomato sauce	1
2 cups	fish stock or water	500 mL
1 cup	dry white wine	250 mL
1/4 cup	chopped fresh parsley	50 mL
Pinch	each dried thyme and oregano	Pinch
1	bay leaf	1
2 lb	clams and/or mussels	1 kg
1 lb	raw fish chunks	500 g
8 oz	raw shrimp, peeled and deveined (optional)	250 g
	Salt and pepper	

● In large heavy saucepan, heat oil over medium heat; cook onions and garlic, stirring occasionally, for about 5 minutes or until softened but not browned. Add tomatoes, tomato sauce, fish stock, wine, half of the parsley, thyme, oregano and bay leaf; simmer for 30 minutes.

● Scrub clams and/or mussels under running water, discarding any that do not close when tapped. Add to pot; cover and cook for 3 minutes. Add fish chunks, and shrimp (if using). Add water if needed to cover fish.

● Simmer for 5 minutes or until fish is opaque. Discard any clams or mussels that do not open. Season with salt and pepper to taste. Ladle into warmed bowls; sprinkle with remaining parsley. Makes 6 servings.

Show off the day's catch from the market or seaside in this streamlined fisherman's stew. It's an impressive but easy and indulgent one-pot feast, ideal for year-round entertaining.

Per serving: about
- 235 calories
- 10 g fat
- excellent source of iron
- 19 g protein
- 16 g carbohydrate

Seafood Gumbo

1/4 cup	vegetable oil	50 mL
1/2 cup	all-purpose flour	125 mL
2	onions, chopped	2
3	cloves garlic, minced	3
2	stalks celery, chopped	2
2 cups	chopped seeded tomatoes	500 mL
1-1/2 tsp	each dried thyme and basil	7 mL
1 tsp	dried oregano	5 mL
1/4 tsp	cayenne pepper	1 mL
2	bay leaves	2
2 cups	fish stock	500 mL
1/2 cup	clam juice	125 mL
8 oz	firm-fleshed fish, cut in chunks	250 g
1	each sweet red and green pepper, chopped	1
8 oz	raw shrimp, peeled and deveined	250 g
8 oz	scallops or cleaned mussels	250 g
6	green onions, sliced	6

● In large heavy saucepan, heat oil over medium-high heat; gradually whisk in flour and cook, whisking, for about 3 minutes or until beginning to darken. Reduce heat to medium; cook, whisking, for about 3 minutes longer or until butterscotch color.

● Add onions, garlic, celery, tomatoes, thyme, basil, oregano, cayenne and bay leaves. Increase heat to medium-high; cook, stirring, for 3 minutes. Gradually whisk in fish stock and clam juice; bring to boil. Reduce heat and simmer for 5 minutes.

● Add fish and red and green peppers; cover and cook for about 5 minutes or until fish is almost opaque.

● Add shrimp and scallops; cook, covered and stirring once gently, for about 5 minutes or until shrimp are pink and scallops are opaque. Discard bay leaves. Ladle into warmed bowls; sprinkle with green onions. Makes 6 servings.

Clam juice adds that extra boost of seafood flavor to a lusty Louisiana specialty. Choose fish that holds its shape while cooking — monkfish, halibut, sea bass, even salmon. Serve over rice.

Per serving: about
- 270 calories
- 11 g fat
- good source of iron
- 22 g protein
- 20 g carbohydrate

Hearty Fish Stew ◄

1 tbsp	olive oil	15 mL
2	onions, chopped	2
3 cups	sliced mushrooms (8 oz/250 g)	750 mL
1	sweet green pepper, chopped	1
6	cloves garlic, minced	6
1	can (28 oz/796 mL) stewed tomatoes, chopped	1
1 cup	chicken or vegetable stock	250 mL
2	potatoes, peeled and diced	2
1 tsp	dried thyme (or 1 tbsp/ 15 mL chopped fresh)	5 mL
1 tsp	salt	5 mL
1/2 tsp	hot pepper sauce	2 mL
1/4 tsp	pepper	1 mL
1-1/2 lb	fish fillets (cod, haddock, sole)	750 g
2 tbsp	chopped fresh parsley	25 mL
1 tbsp	grated lemon rind	15 mL

● In large heavy saucepan, heat oil over medium heat; cook onions, stirring occasionally, for 5 minutes or until softened. Add mushrooms, green pepper and two-thirds of the garlic; cook, stirring occasionally, for 10 minutes or until softened.

● Add tomatoes, chicken stock, potatoes, thyme, salt, hot pepper sauce and pepper; bring to simmer. Cover and simmer for 10 minutes or until potatoes are almost tender.

● Cut fish into 1-inch (2.5 cm) chunks; add to pan and cook for 3 to 5 minutes or until fish flakes easily when tested with fork.

● Meanwhile, in bowl, stir together parsley, lemon rind and remaining garlic. Ladle stew into warmed bowls; sprinkle with parsley mixture. Makes 4 servings.

The tempting aromas of mushrooms, tomatoes, garlic and thyme will bring everyone to the table to enjoy fish in a new and quick weeknight way.

Per serving: about
- 340 calories
- 6 g fat
- excellent source of iron
- 37 g protein
- 38 g carbohydrate
- very high source of fiber

WHEN YOU DON'T HAVE WHAT YOU NEED

Nowhere are substitutions and alternatives more appropriate than in soups and stews. Here are some good ones. Note that the dish made with a substitute will not taste exactly the same, but it will taste good. However, avoid using a substitute for a major ingredient. What's a spinach soup without spinach or a chicken cacciatore without mushrooms!

● Spinach can replace Swiss chard and beet greens. It can often replace kale and collards, but reduce cooking time.

● No leeks or shallots? Use regular onions.

● Firm squash stands in for sweet potatoes; regular potatoes can replace sweet.

● Carrots can replace parsnips.

● Sweet red, yellow and orange bell peppers are interchangeable as far as flavor is concerned; they can all be replaced by the less sweet green pepper.

● Instead of chives, use the green part of green onions.

● Frozen, canned and fresh corn kernels are virtually the same in soup and stew recipes. Add frozen or canned corn later in the recipe. Ditto, fresh and frozen peas.

● Stock, preferably unsalted, can replace up to 1 cup (250 mL) wine. Add 1 tbsp (15 mL) red or white wine vinegar for a bit of the authentic wine bite.

● Almost all dried beans (canned) can be used interchangeably, and can replace chick-peas if needed.

● Red wine vinegar and a pinch of sugar will do for balsamic vinegar. Cider vinegar with a pinch of granulated sugar will do for rice wine vinegar.

● Olive oil, although not as tasty, is acceptable for extra virgin olive oil, and vegetable oil will do for both, although you should add just a little more herbs to make up for the olive flavor.

● Olive and vegetable oils can replace butter when sautéeing vegetables for soups and stews.

● Pearl and pot barley are interchangeable in soups and stews.

● Parboiled long grain rice, regular long grain rice and basmati rice fill the same function, but basmati is tastier and parboiled cooks up with perfect separate grains.

● Fresh herbs can be replaced by dried herbs, usually in the ratio of 3 fresh to 1 dried.

● Chicken and fish stock can be replaced by vegetable stock, especially when making recipes vegetarian.

Curried Mussels with Ginger ▶

Although there is a touch of exotic ginger and curry, this recipe also traces its roots to France. Slice plenty of crusty bread for dunking.

Per serving: about
- 345 calories
- 10 g protein
- 29 g fat
- 9 g carbohydrate
- good source of iron

2 lb	mussels	1 kg
2 tbsp	vegetable oil	25 mL
1	onion, finely chopped	1
2	cloves garlic, minced	2
2 tsp	minced gingerroot	10 mL
1 tbsp	curry powder	15 mL
1/2 cup	dry white wine or clam juice	125 mL
1 cup	whipping cream	250 mL
	Salt and pepper	
2 tbsp	chopped fresh coriander or green onion	25 mL

● Just before cooking, scrub mussels with stiff brush or nylon pad under cold running water. Remove byssus (beard) attached to shell by pulling up toward rounded end of shell, or by cutting off. Discard any mussels with cracked shells or any that don't close when tapped. Set aside.

● In large heavy saucepan, heat oil over medium heat; cook onion, garlic and ginger, stirring occasionally, for 3 minutes or until softened. Add curry powder; cook, stirring, for 30 seconds. Pour in wine; bring to simmer over medium-high heat.

● Add mussels; cover and cook for 5 to 7 minutes or until mussels open, shaking pan occasionally to redistribute mussels. With slotted spoon, remove mussels and keep warm, discarding any that do not open.

● Bring liquid in pan to boil over high heat; boil for about 3 minutes or until reduced to 1/2 cup (125 mL). Pour in cream; boil for about 2 minutes or until thick enough to coat back of wooden spoon. Season with salt and pepper to taste.

● Transfer mussels to warmed bowls. Pour sauce over top; sprinkle with coriander. Makes 4 servings.

VARIATION
● MUSSELS IN WINE AND HERBS: In large heavy saucepan, melt 2 tbsp (25 mL) butter over medium heat; cook 1 finely chopped onion or shallot and 2 minced cloves garlic for 2 to 4 minutes or until softened. Add 1-1/2 cups (375 mL) white wine; bring to boil and boil for 4 minutes. Add mussels; cover and boil for 4 minutes or until opened, shaking pan occasionally. Remove mussels to bowls. To pan, add 2 tbsp (25 mL) chopped green onion, 1 tbsp (15 mL) chopped fresh dill, and salt and pepper to taste; pour over mussels.

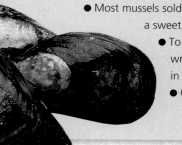

BUYING AND STORING MUSSELS
● Most mussels sold today are cultivated and are sand-and-grit-free. Choose clean, shiny ones with a sweet, fresh smell. Shells should be tightly closed or close when tapped.
● To store live mussels, refrigerate for up to 24 hours in open container with well wrung-out wet towel over top; mussels need air and moisture but must not sit in water.
● Clean mussels just before cooking.

Ratatouille ▶

Summer wouldn't be complete without at least one pot of Provençale-inspired ratatouille simmering on the stove. Get in lots of sourdough baguette to mop up the lusty juices.

Per serving: about
• 135 calories
• 7 g fat
• high source of fiber
• 3 g protein
• 17 g carbohydrate

1	eggplant (12 oz/375 g)	1
3	small zucchini (12 oz/375 g total)	3
1-1/2 tsp	salt	7 mL
1/4 cup	olive oil	50 mL
3	large cloves garlic, minced	3
1	Spanish onion, thinly sliced	1
2	large sweet green peppers, cut in 1-inch (2.5 cm) chunks	2
1	large sweet red or yellow pepper, cut in 1-inch (2.5 cm) chunks	1
6	large tomatoes (2 lb/1 kg total)	6
3 tbsp	chopped fresh basil (or 1-1/2 tsp/7 mL dried)	50 mL
2 tbsp	chopped fresh marjoram (or 1-1/2 tsp/7 mL dried)	25 mL
1/2 tsp	granulated sugar	2 mL
1/4 tsp	pepper	1 mL
Pinch	cayenne pepper	Pinch

● Cut eggplant and zucchini into 1-inch (2.5 cm) cubes. Layer in colander, sprinkling with 1 tsp (5 mL) of the salt; let drain for 30 minutes. Rinse and transfer to towels; pat dry.

● In large heavy saucepan, heat half of the oil with the garlic over medium heat. Add onion; cook, stirring, for 1 minute. Add green and red peppers; cook, stirring, for 1 minute. Repeat with eggplant, then zucchini, then tomatoes, cooking each for 1 minute.

● Sprinkle with remaining oil and salt, basil, marjoram, sugar, pepper and cayenne. Reduce heat, cover and simmer, stirring occasionally, for 40 minutes. Uncover and cook for 15 to 20 minutes longer or until liquid is reduced slightly and vegetables are tender. Makes 8 servings.

Skillet Vegetable Stew

There's fiber, color and extra taste in potato, zucchini and eggplant skins, so peel only if they're tough or blemished.

Per serving: about
• 240 calories
• 6 g fat
• good source of iron
• 8 g protein
• 43 g carbohydrate
• very high source of fiber

1 tbsp	olive oil	15 mL
Half	onion, sliced	Half
3	tomatoes, coarsely chopped	3
1-1/2 tsp	salt	7 mL
1 tsp	each dried basil and pepper	5 mL
4	red potatoes, cut in 1/2-inch (1 cm) cubes	4
1	sweet red or green pepper, chopped	1
2 cups	each cubed eggplant and zucchini	500 mL
1/4 cup	chopped fresh parsley	50 mL
1/4 cup	freshly grated Parmesan cheese	50 mL

● In large nonstick skillet, heat oil over medium heat; cook onion, stirring occasionally, for 5 minutes. Add tomatoes, salt, basil and pepper; cover and cook for 5 minutes.

● Add potatoes, 1/4 cup (50 mL) water and red pepper; bring to boil. Reduce heat, cover and simmer for 10 minutes. Stir in eggplant; simmer, covered and stirring occasionally, for 10 minutes.

● Add zucchini; cook, covered, for about 5 minutes or until zucchini is tender-crisp and other vegetables are tender. Stir in parsley. Serve sprinkled with cheese. Makes 4 servings.

TIP: If you have fresh basil, use 1/4 cup (50 mL) chopped instead of the dried basil and fresh parsley.

Artichoke and Chick-Pea Stew

*O*ne real advantage to
vegetarian stews is a short
cooking time. Even with a
long list of ingredients, this
six-serving stew can be ready
in less than an hour.

Per serving: about
- 320 calories
- 13 g fat
- good source
  of iron
- 10 g protein
- 45 g carbohydrate
- very high source
  of fiber

2 tbsp	olive oil	25 mL
2	onions, chopped	2
3	cloves garlic, minced	3
1 tsp	dried thyme	5 mL
1/2 tsp	each turmeric, cinnamon and ginger	2 mL
Pinch	each salt and pepper	Pinch
3 tbsp	all-purpose flour	50 mL
2	sweet potatoes, peeled and cubed	2
1	can (19 oz/540 mL) chick-peas, drained and rinsed	1
1	sweet red pepper, cubed	1
1	can (19 oz/540 mL) tomatoes, chopped	1
3 cups	vegetable stock	750 mL
1	can (14 oz/398 mL) artichoke hearts, drained and quartered	1
1/2 cup	oil-cured black olives	125 mL
2 tbsp	lemon juice	25 mL
1/4 cup	chopped fresh coriander or parsley	50 mL
1/4 cup	sliced almonds, toasted	50 mL

● In large heavy saucepan, heat oil over
medium heat. Add onions, garlic, thyme,
turmeric, cinnamon, ginger, salt and pepper;
cover and cook, stirring occasionally, for
5 minutes or until softened. Sprinkle with
flour; cook, stirring, for 1 minute.

● Stir in potatoes, chick-peas, red pepper,
tomatoes and vegetable stock; bring to boil.
Reduce heat and simmer, stirring
occasionally, for about 30 minutes or until
vegetables are just tender.

● Stir in artichoke hearts, olives and lemon
juice; simmer for 10 minutes or until
vegetables are very tender. Gently stir in
coriander. Serve garnished with almonds.
Makes 6 servings.

Chock-full of Vegetables Chili

*F*rom Heartburn Day, a
Stratford, Ontario, fundraiser
chili lunch for the Heart and
Stroke Foundation, comes
this colorful and inexpensive
vegetarian chili.

Per serving: about
- 230 calories
- 4 g fat
- excellent
  source of iron
- 12 g protein
- 42 g carbohydrate
- very high
  source of fiber

1 tbsp	vegetable oil	15 mL
2 tbsp	chili powder	25 mL
1 tbsp	dried oregano	15 mL
1 tsp	each ground cumin and coriander	5 mL
1 tsp	each salt and pepper	5 mL
1	large sweet red or green pepper, chopped	1
1	large red onion, chopped	1
3	stalks celery, sliced	3
3	large cloves garlic, minced	3
1/2 cup	each green and red lentils	125 mL
1	can (19 oz/540 mL) tomatoes	1
3 cups	cubed peeled butternut squash	750 mL

● In large heavy saucepan, heat oil over
medium heat; cook chili powder, oregano,
cumin, coriander, salt and pepper, stirring,
for 1 minute. Add red pepper, onion, celery
and garlic; cook, stirring occasionally, for
about 6 minutes or until softened.

● Meanwhile, sort green and red lentils,
discarding any discolored ones; rinse and
drain. Add lentils to pan; cook, stirring, for
3 minutes. Add 4 cups (1 L) water; bring to
boil. Reduce heat to low; cover and simmer
for 15 minutes or until vegetables are tender
and green lentils begin to soften.

● Add tomatoes, breaking up with spoon.
Add squash; cover and simmer, stirring
often, for 30 minutes or until tender and
liquid is thickened. Makes 6 servings.

Curried Vegetables

4	carrots	4
4	parsnips	4
2	potatoes	2
8 oz	green beans	250 g
1 tbsp	vegetable oil	15 mL
1	onion, chopped	1
2	cloves garlic, minced	2
1 tbsp	minced gingerroot	15 mL
2 tsp	ground coriander	10 mL
1-1/2 tsp	ground cumin	7 mL
1/2 tsp	each cinnamon and turmeric	2 mL
1/4 tsp	each salt and pepper	1 mL
Pinch	hot pepper flakes	Pinch
1 cup	vegetable stock	250 mL
1 cup	coconut milk	250 mL

● Peel and cut carrots and parsnips into 1/2-inch (1 cm) thick diagonal slices. Peel and cube potatoes. Cut green beans into 1-inch (2.5 cm) lengths. Set vegetables aside.

● In large heavy saucepan, heat oil over medium heat; cook carrots, parsnips, onion, garlic, ginger, coriander, cumin, cinnamon, turmeric, salt, pepper and hot pepper flakes, stirring often, for 5 minutes or until softened.

● Pour in vegetable stock and coconut milk; bring to boil. Add potatoes and green beans; reduce heat to medium, cover and cook for about 10 minutes or until vegetables are almost tender. Uncover and cook for about 5 minutes or until all vegetables are tender. Makes 4 servings.

Serve this chunky curry over rice — basmati is the most enticing because of its natural aroma and flavor — and add a few crisp poppadams (wafer-thin pieces of flatbread), a dollop of thick yogurt and a dab of mango chutney.

Per serving: about
- 385 calories
- 17 g fat
- excellent source of iron
- 7 g protein
- 58 g carbohydrate
- very high source of fiber

Vegetarian Gumbo

1	buttercup squash (about 1-1/2 lb/750 g	1
3 tbsp	vegetable oil	50 mL
1/3 cup	all-purpose flour	75 mL
2	onions, sliced	2
3	cloves garlic, minced	3
2	stalks celery, chopped	2
1 tsp	dried thyme	5 mL
1/2 tsp	each pepper and hot pepper flakes	2 mL
4 cups	vegetable stock	1 L
1-1/2 cups	crushed tomatoes	375 mL
3 cups	shredded greens (such as spinach, kale, beet greens)	750 mL
1	can (19 oz/540 mL) red kidney beans, drained and rinsed	1
1 cup	fresh or frozen green peas	250 mL

● Peel and seed squash; cut into chunks. Set aside.

● In large heavy saucepan, heat oil over medium-high heat; whisk in flour and cook, whisking, for about 3 minutes or until beginning to darken. Reduce heat to medium; cook, whisking, for 3 minutes longer or until butterscotch color.

● Add onions, garlic and celery; cook, stirring, for 3 minutes or until softened. Add thyme, pepper and hot pepper flakes; cook, stirring, for 1 minute.

● Add vegetable stock, tomatoes and squash; bring to boil. Reduce heat and simmer, stirring occasionally, for 10 to 15 minutes or until squash is tender. Add greens, kidney beans and peas; cover and cook for about 5 minutes or until greens are wilted and all vegetables are tender. Makes 8 servings.

There's a touch of heat in this red bean and vegetable stew that starts, like all gumbos, by cooking flour and oil together until they become butterscotch brown and flavorful. Rice is a must with any gumbo.

Per serving: about
- 210 calories
- 6 g fat
- good source of iron
- 8 g protein
- 32 g carbohydrate
- very high source of fiber

The Contributors

Photography Credits

FRED BIRD: pages 39, 42, 52, 55, 75, 85.

DOUGLAS BRADSHAW: pages 4, 11, 51, 56, 76, 82.

ELLEN BRODYLO and MICHAEL MORROW: page 14.

PETER CHOU: pages 40, 64.

VINCENT NOGUCHI: page 68.

JOY VON TIEDEMANN: page 24.

ROBERT WIGINGTON: front cover; pages 3, 7, 8, 17, 18, 19, 21, 23, 27, 30, 33, 34, 36, 45, 49, 59, 60, 66, 73, 79, 87.

In the Canadian Living Test Kitchen. From left: Susan Van Hezewijk, Donna Bartolini (Test Kitchen manager), Jennifer MacKenzie, Daphna Rabinovitch (associate food director) and Elizabeth Baird (food director). Absent from photo: Heather Howe and Emily Richards.

Special Thanks

My thanks to the great team of soup and stew makers at *Canadian Living* who prepared the contents of *Canadian Living's Best Soups and Stews* — especially associate food director Daphna Rabinovitch, who worked with Test Kitchen home economist Susan Van Hezewijk in the creation of new recipes. Thanks also to the rest of the Test Kitchen staff under manager Donna Bartolini: Heather Howe, Jennifer MacKenzie and Emily Richards, and to our valued food writers (noted on p. 90). Managing editor Susan Antonacci, senior editor Julia Armstrong, editorial assistant Olga Goncalves, plus the art department under Cate Cochran and copy department under Michael Killingsworth, personify the excellence in initial preparation of the food pages for *Canadian Living*. Senior editor Beverley Renahan wears two hats in all *Canadian Living* cookbooks — first as meticulous senior editor in the magazine's food department, and secondly in an even more meticulous copy editing of the recipes for book publication. Thanks are extended to editor-in-chief Bonnie Cowan and publisher Caren King for their support in expanding *Canadian Living* beyond the pages of the magazine.

There are others to thank, too. On the visual side — our photographers (noted above); plus prop stylists Maggi Jones, Janet Walkinshaw, Shelly Tauber, Bridget Sargeant and Susan Doherty-Hannaford, who provided the backgrounds, dishes and embellishments for the sets; and food stylists Kate Bush, Ruth Gangbar, Debbi Charendoff Moses, Lucie Richard, Olga Truchan, Jennifer McLagan, Jill Snider, Sharon Dale and Kathy Robertson, who make the food look good enough to eat — right off the page.

Book designers Gord Sibley and Dale Vokey are responsible for the splendid design of the *Best* series.

Great appreciation goes to Madison Press Books' associate editorial director, Wanda Nowakowska, who manages to make each of the *Best* books special and unique. Help from Tina Gaudino and others at Madison Press is always appreciated. At Random House, members of the marketing and publicity department — Kathy Bain, Pat Cairns, Sheila Kay and Cathy Paine — deserve sincere thanks, as does Duncan Shields, the indefatigable mass marketing sales manager (Ballantine Books). I appreciate the support for the *Canadian Living* cookbooks from president and publisher of Random House, David Kent, and Madison Press Books president Albert Cummings.

Elizabeth Baird

Index

Over 100 delicious soups, stews and other bowlfuls worth savoring.

Look to
CANADIAN LIVING
for all
BEST!
of the

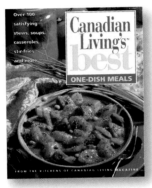

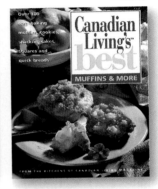

Watch for more new books in the months ahead...
from Canadian Living so you know they're —THE BEST!